Nurture Your Child's Gift

Inspired Parenting

Nurture Your Child's Gift
Inspired Parenting

Caron B. Goode, Ed.D.

BEYOND
WORDS
Publishing
I N C

Beyond Words Publishing, Inc.
20827 N.W. Cornell Road, Suite 500
Hillsboro, Oregon 97124-9808
503-531-8700
1-800-284-9673

Managing editor: Julie Steigerwaldt
Proofreader: Marvin Moore
Design: Principia Graphica and Dorral Lukas
Composition: William H. Brunson Typography Services
Printed in the United States of America
Distributed to the book trade by Publishers Group West

Library of Congress Cataloging-in-Publication Data
Goode, Caron B.
    Nurture your child's gift : inspired parenting / Caron B. Goode.
      p. cm.
    ISBN 1-58270-040-0 (paperback)
    1. Parenting.   2. Child development.   3. Self-esteem in children.
I. Title.
HQ755.8 .G665   2001
649'.1—dc21

                                            00-064214

The corporate mission of Beyond Words Publishing, Inc.:
Inspire to Integrity

To Michelle Reynolds.

*She was a nurturing mother to Kyle and Garrett and also cared
for many of the world's children through her work,
inspiring each of us to appreciate our children's unique gifts.*

She passed from this world in 1999 after a battle with leukemia.

Contents

Contents

Acknowledgments to Contributing Authors

Several individuals have contributed their wisdom, professional expertise, and personal experiences to the making of this book. For their active professional collaboration in specific subjects covered in this book, I gratefully and wholeheartedly acknowledge them with a summary of their professional qualifications and other accomplishments. Published titles appear in the notes and the resources.

Self-Esteem: **Michelle Reynolds** held a Master's in international communications. She consulted with a number of regional, national, and international nonprofit organizations concerned with children's and youth issues. Reynolds was a freelance writer and editor who lived in Lakewood, N.Y., with her husband and two sons, Kyle and Garrett. She died in 1999 after a battle with leukemia.

Empowerment: **Joy Watson**, a human development educator, holds degrees in sociology/psychology and speech and language pathology (M.Ed.). She has worked professionally as an international consultant in business, education, and health, conducting seminars and designing communication programs to maximize human potential, communication, personal and team success, and wellness. As a principal consultant of Mind Fitness™ International, she developed the integrated education-health technology Mind Fitness™. She has authored books on Mind Fitness including *Twenty Minutes to Sanity* and *The Upside of Being Down*. She is presently doing stone and bronze sculpting and lives in Jackson Hole, Wyoming.

Mindbody Connection: **Donna Packard, M.Ed.,** has studied the mindbody connection for the past twenty years. She is a Certified Transformational Facilitator of the International Breath Institute, a certified educational kinesiologist, has extensive knowledge and experience in utilizing sound and color in learning and healing, and has developed and facilitated numerous experiential workshops. These include "Using Sound in Learning and Healing," "The Human Energy Field," "Stress Management," "Guided Imagery," "Alcohol Awareness," "Making Your Dreams Come True," "Breathwork," and motivational programs. Packard has worked extensively with homeless families and with individual parents and children. She has worked in alcohol and drug rehabilitation programs teaching and counseling people from all walks of life in areas of self-empowerment, literacy, and life skills. She is an artist, writer, and musician. Through her private practice, Packard facilitates groups and individuals toward achieving a greater sense of well-being and living each moment more fully.

Breath: **Tom Goode, N.D.,** left a successful corporate career following a miracle healing of a progressive, degenerative disease. Sharing with others what he learned about holistic and alternative approaches to wellness, he began a private healing/counseling practice in 1977. He received his doctorate in naturopathic medicine in 1992 and is the founder and president of the International Breath Institute, which offers health and wellness programs and professional certification in the use of Full Wave Breathing™ and the TEMS (TransformBreathing™ Energy Management System) program throughout the United States and in Australia.

Music: **Dorothea Joyce** is a professional performer and award-winning songwriter. She majored in piano and voice at Indiana University School of Music and received her B.S. in music education from Wayne State University, after which she served as the music-department head for a private school designing integrated and innovative music programs. She received her M.A. in music therapy from New York University, after which she designed therapeutic family musical programs for communication, cooperation, bonding, and changes in family dynamics.

Her song "Love's Lines, Angles, and Rhymes," recorded by the Fifth Dimension, was certified a Gold Record. Added to her credits are a Clio in advertising for her jingle music and lyrics "Laire du Temps Perfume," and a Cannes Film Festival Winner for the best song in a film (*Jeremy*). She was twice elected to the board of the Songwriters Guild of America and is a member of ASCAP as well as NARAS (The Grammy Awards), having served on the committee called "Grammy's in the Schools," a program of celebrity performance in New York public schools.

Joyce has extensive experience in the human-potential movement. Currently, she holds "Seminars in Concert for Inner Peace." She also has a consulting service called "Seeded Signatures" to help parents design the physical and sound environments in their children's rooms. Her CDs and layouts can be viewed and ordered through *www.mach1audio.com.dorothea* or by calling 1-888-REJOICE.

Preface

*You are wholly complete and your success in life will be in direct
proportion to your ability to accept this truth about you.*

Dr. Robert Anthony

Such a plethora of parenting information graces our book-
shelves. *Why this book?* Within the spheres of my parenting experiences and professional roles, I discovered a large gap. Space
exists between mindbody research and the ease that these techniques can bring to our parenting roles. Imagine the simplicity
of playing a piece of music to help a child mentally focus or of
guiding children in breathing deeper and fuller to help them
calm down and manage stress. And how about acting out the
solutions to arguments or drawing a treasure map of sequential
steps to complete a task? *Nurture Your Child's Gift* can help us simplify our parenting roles and ease our personal anxiety about
doing it "right."

Indeed, new educational techniques, research in the psychology of emotions and temperaments, as well as psycho-
immunology studies show us the phenomenal, intrinsic links
between the mind and the body. We can no longer hold
the Cartesian view of the body as a mechanical processor.
Rather, the mindbody system is a dynamic processor of energy
seen in cell-to-cell communication throughout every organ
and system.

Why me? In each step of my career, I've been challenged by
these questions:

- ☞ What is the best way to teach this child?
- ☞ How can I motivate this youth?
- ☞ How can I demonstrate to this youngster how to approach an overwhelming task?
- ☞ What is the best way to handle an overactive, sick, gifted, or maladaptive student?
- ☞ How can I assist parents to define boundaries as well as expectations for children?
- ☞ How can family members show kindness and compassion to each other?
- ☞ How can I help parents decide when to protect or encourage their child?
- ☞ How can I help children cope and relax with increasing stressors—high expectations, media bombardment, hours of computer and television, and performance anxiety?

I learned the same truths that you are learning—that my pictures of what teachers *should do* and my expectations about who good parents *ought to be* don't work. Change happens! Life goes on! So how can we depend on our rules, expectations, and someone's invisible laws about how to rear, motivate, and coach children to success? The parenting choice in any given moment comes from our emotions, gut-level feelings, and how we happen to be feeling. What if we could manage our emotions, trust our intuition, and feel good about the choices we make at least 90 percent of the time? This book will help you do that.

When my thoughts, expectations, and rules about how it ought to be dissolved through life's experience and interactions, I was left with this awareness:

- The present moment
- The heart of the matter
- The context of the situation
- The question "What will work best here?"

I learned that being in my heart, observing the situation, and allowing the answer to emerge worked better than trying to remember teaching techniques or counseling protocol. Because I worked with so many people in crisis, like every parent experiences at times, I learned to take a deeper breath, watch the undercurrent, and seek closure, communication, or an action step.

In these parenting moments of life, we can't always recall the logic of why we acted as we did. It was emotion, intuition, perception, a mistake, and an opportunity to watch and choose a response. We don't say, "I remember where I read it." We more often say, " I was just there, and success happened!"

Those special moments of staying in our hearts, observing context, and choosing our responses are explained by science and psychology as mindbody medicine. Calmness is easily achieved. Learning to be aware of interactions is recognized as an intelligence. Intuition and common sense are valued as much as logic and intellect. The power of parenting is being returned to you through the biochemistry of thought and emotions. We can actually teach children how to manage their thoughts and emotions using the suggestions throughout this book.

Why now? It is time to support children's gifts for their personal happiness and achievement. It's time to enable each child to find and fulfill his dream. The reason has been said hundreds of different ways throughout the thirty years of my work with children of all ages, normal and disabling conditions, as well as families in need of care and calm communication.

- ☞ "I gotta like something to do it, you know."
- ☞ "Why should I care about life if I'm not gonna do what I came here to do?"
- ☞ "Everybody needs a dream, Teach. Or we're living blind!"
- ☞ "Why don't you show me how to do something great instead of this classwork?"
- ☞ "My dream gives me hope. That's why I got beyond my (abuse, disability, pain, and illness)."
- ☞ "If we don't have something bigger than ourselves to hold on to, then why bother?"
- ☞ "Where's the meaning?"
- ☞ "Give me something to care about."

These are the challenges of our children's generation. A talent or gift, a dream, a vision for a life brings hope. It's simple enough. No destination—no road map. No passion or motivation—no success or achievement. No mentor, friend, role model, or parent—no one to reflect the belief, dream, hope, or success.

If we are too hurt, hurried, busied, reactive, stressed out, numb, rushed, negative, or sick, then we need to change. Life will simply pass us by as we *think* we are living it!

On the other hand, we'll participate in the flow of life when we can watch, laugh, respond, express, and know what our dream is. Our raison d'être surfaces at various times in childhood. Our dream teases us to keep our interest and skills sharp and invites us to achieve and succeed! Our dreams can flourish when we use our God-given talents and resources. This book can show you how to do this for yourself as well as for your child.

As you use this book as a reference to help your children manage their thoughts and emotions to develop their gifts and achieve their dreams, you will too. And it's absolutely wonderful!

Introduction

Nurture Your Child's Gift calls for a revolution. It upsets the comfortable, fundamental assumptions about the way we engage our children and foster their development. Nurture Your Child's Gift asks us to see our children as living souls who come to this world with a unique gift and dream to fulfill. Their life journey can be the discovery and expression of that vision. If we knew that our children were our planetary and societal salvation and held the answer to the questions of how to survive and thrive into the next century, how would we treat them? This book provides an answer.

Dr. Caron Goode

A PARENTING REVOLUTION

Collectively, the statistics regarding our children's state of consciousness are frightening. Research shows a worldwide trend of increased suicide, depression, and loneliness. Stress in children as well as aggression, worry, eating disorders, and learning impairments are high. New studies in the United States indicate growing violence and antisocial behaviors in our schools. The trends, however, are global—transcending culture, society, school, religions, and family.

In our efforts to see that our children survive in today's world, we have denied their individuality. We've asked them to do what appears safe rather than what their heart truly desires. In addition, many have lost hope. How can this trend be changed?

To make this happen, a parenting revolution is called for in the way we view and treat our children, especially if we want them to reach their full potential, make their unique contribution to society, and find satisfaction, fulfillment, and joy in life.

A WHOLE-CHILD APPROACH

We have become fragmented in our worldview and developed segmented disciplines in our society: medicine treats the body; psychology deals with the mind; education trains the intellect; and religion cares for the soul. However, in the last fifteen years the field of psychoneuroimmunology has demonstrated that the mind and body are one system and the components cannot be isolated from one another. To do so creates disorder.

The concept of wholeness has combined the various disciplines and presents a menu of options from which parents can choose appropriate techniques to assist their children in the skills required to successfully recognize their gift and live their dream. In the institutions of higher learning, we have

- Constructed new theories of intelligence and emotional development of children
- Mapped the emotions in the body
- Discovered where thoughts are anchored in the brain tissue

- Observed how the stress chemical, cortisol, hosts a trail of symptoms that predict ill health
- Learned how appropriate breathing can assuage the stress symptoms
- Demonstrated how music can soothe emotions and relax the heart
- Proven that when we can express ourselves in a variety of modalities such as movement, art, dancing, or sculpture, we feel better and function more effectively
- Documented the effectiveness of mindbody technologies about which the National Institutes of Health reported in its 1992 *Report on Alternative Medicine.*[1]

Nurture Your Child's Gift assists parents by providing the latest information for a whole-child approach to empowering the dream. It shares mindbody advances from such fields as medicine, sports, psychology, and education and applies them directly to developing our children's esteem, empowerment, and expression, the building blocks of dream making. The techniques can be as simple as playing the right piece of music to soothe ruffled emotions and as natural as taking a deep breath to ease stress symptoms.

THE DREAM-VISION FOR LIFE

Children who have vision find their joy in life. They have realized their gift, touched their creative core, and found their dream.

The dream in each person's heart steers the course of his or her life. It sparks one's passion for being alive. The dream unfolds and refines its expression throughout childhood, adolescence, and beyond. Following one's inner direction, however, is often discouraged by society in general and our educational system in particular, both of which value conformity. We must revolutionize our view of parenting to support rather than deny the dream.

The dream is a vision of innate potential, of the natural gifts that our children bring with them into this world. Experts used to believe that children entered this world *tabula rasa*, a blank slate. Yet any parent or person who has worked with children knows that each child, when nurtured and encouraged, develops according to his or her unique temperament and abilities. If accorded supportive life circumstances, a child will fulfill that specific dream or particular life task.

The authors contributing to *Nurture Your Child's Gift* believe that the vision in every child needs to be recognized and encouraged. This requires a daring and bold response. We as parents need a collective agreement to no longer see our children as unknowing beings to be impressed and programmed with society's traditional culture and limitations. Rather, to find our child's gift and nurture the dream requires the highest kind of love—one that is volitional—based on the child's needs and potentials. It requires effort to observe, learn, make mistakes, perform re-takes, and be conscious of our modeling. It is, however, the loving way that we have all asked for.

Gifts and dreams take time to emerge in any individual. We can, however, encourage them to reveal their identity through specific mindbody techniques that foster emotional openness, increase physical relaxation, and develop intelligence and intuition.

For example, think of the human mind and body as an energy loop. In optimal conditions, energy flows freely throughout the bodily systems. If we are surrounded by intense negativity, are stressed out, or experience trauma, the loop gets blocked and paralyzes us in some way. Blocked energy shows up in our children as their being "tuned-out" from stress and mentally distracted or depressed. Their emotions may take wide swings. They feel stuck, frozen, paralyzed, angry, intense, or inert. They develop attention deficits and learning disorders.

On the other hand, when we are "in the flow," our energy is open. We feel good, energized, fluid, inspired, expectant, trusting, animated, invigorated, and enlivened. The wholistic applications of breathwork, music, creative problem solving, self-dialogue, affirmation, and imagery assist children to harmonize their mind-body system.

We can change the world, one remarkable family at a time. *Nurture Your Child's Gift* advances a revolution in child rearing—in the way we think about and act toward our children. It provides easy and natural approaches to realizing children's gifts and dreams.

WHOLE-CHILD PARENTING

What empowers successful parents? It's the ability to observe or see what works or what doesn't work and the flexibility to change course. *This is called awareness or mindfulness in our daily life.*

For instance, our parenting is not as simple as black and white, good or bad, or right or wrong choices. We can convey through our language and actions that we all have several choices in any situation. By learning to be mindful and aware of what we put into action, both parents and children can learn to make choices that work. Too, rather than labeling and belaboring mistakes, we can take basketball coach Jim Harrick's words to heart. He says, "The team that makes the most mistakes will generally win the game."

To be a parent means to make mistakes, but we don't have to take them personally. *A sense of humor and a dose of love are what we call parenting with heart.* This book emphasizes an openhearted parenting style that helps a family laugh together, learn from each other, breathe together, enjoy music with each other, and look at life through a creative lens.

Nurture Your Child's Gift speaks to whole-child parenting as a revolutionary approach to move us beyond our comfort zone, to stretch for our children's visions, and to support our children's gifts. Esteem and empowerment are the building blocks for the dream's expression and help children achieve their personal success. This book documents the research in support of mindbody technologies for child rearing and moves away from conventional education. We want to inspire parents and children to creatively express themselves and learn to appropriately manage their emotions and thoughts.

The sections of this book called "Reflections" are to help parents remember their own wholeness, unique temperament, and personal dream. We encourage you to help yourselves in order to help your children. Use this book as a resource and reference for new ways to approach parenting when you feel stuck. To encourage the revolution in the way that we think, buy another copy of this book and present it to a friend.

The child who is a visionary or dreamer will be a maverick. He or she will also be a progenitor of ideas and creativity. These children don't always fit into the conventional systems of education. As parents, we can help and prepare them to use their gifts wisely and share their dreams as global citizens.

Prologue

The Dream

At age seven, Oliver had a dream. Not an ordinary dream—he'd
had plenty of those. This dream was about Oliver's life purpose
and gift, although he didn't know it at the time. Here are his words:

> The first dream that I will remember for the rest of my life was
> one where I was in a mansion. It was sort of a game with four
> other people. We had to get to the attic of the mansion through
> all of these twists and turns and booby traps and survive. The
> point of the game was survival. If you didn't die, you won.
>
> It was the first time I was conscious of a dream being in
> black-and-white. I went through all the booby traps. Other
> people got killed, speared, and lost. I finally made it to the
> top. When I was approaching the attic door, a trapdoor
> opened under me and I started falling.
>
> But I didn't see it through my eyes; I saw it through the
> eyes of a camera. I watched my body fall and fall. I saw
> these spikes underneath me. Then my body just froze in mid-
> air and the credits rolled. I woke up laughing! There were
> credits like at the end of the movie, so I knew I was in a movie.

This dream was the beginning of Oliver's quest to be an actor.
Not an ordinary dream at all. Would Oliver's dream come true?

Part One

Lenses through Which We Can View the Unfolding Dream:

Emotional Patterns,

Temperament,

and Intelligence Clusters

1

Children's Gifts and Dreams

*I have heard it said that the first ingredient of success—the earliest spark
in the dreaming youth—is this: dream a great dream.*
John A. Applema

*Stop trying to perfect your child, but keep trying to perfect
your relationship with him.*
Dr. Henker

Any parent or person who has worked with children knows that
each child is unique from birth, displaying a particular temperament, abilities, and interests. We are all born with these "givens"
or gifts, and it is by honoring this uniqueness and respecting the
emergent dreams of children that we become truly nurturing
parents and adults.

"The dream" is an inner vision of what our lives are about. It
is an imprint in our hearts that steers the course of our lives and,
like Oliver's, points us toward that purpose in our lives.

Dreams spark our passion for being alive. They are like
anchors we hold on to when life seems dark or becomes a struggle. A dream unfolds gradually, refining its expression throughout
childhood and the adolescent years. But how do we recognize the
one dream, among all our dreams, that defines our purpose in life?
► *We can recognize the dream because it will reveal itself, time and again,
through inner prompting, innate ability, and driving interests.*

Often this dream is lost as children grow. Society in general, and our educational system in particular, values conformity rather than following one's inner direction. Don't we want our children to reach their full potential? To find satisfaction and joy in life? Then we must learn new ways of parenting that *support* rather than deny the dream.

Nurture Your Child's Gift shows us how to observe the unfolding dream within children and how to help foster its emergence. We want to watch for it, recognize it as it unfolds, and nurture it.

DREAMS HAVE IMPACT

The Rev. Martin Luther King Jr. displayed great courage when he pronounced, "I have a dream." It takes courage to speak of our dreams. As King stood before a sea of faces that day, he pledged commitment to his heartfelt desire.

What made King's statement so powerful is that he had the courage to acknowledge and follow his dream. Like King putting changes into motion at that historic moment, parents also have the opportunity to change history.

▶ *Helping our children know and unfold their life dream has an impact on our society and on our world that we can barely imagine.*

It is individuals with the courage to live their dreams who have made great contributions to our culture in the areas of the arts, politics, media, science, and spirituality. Visions, dreaming, and creativity were part of their personalities. These qualities were fostered primarily by their personal inner drive, not necessarily by school or family. We are looking for this inner drive in our children. All children have dreams we want to foster.

WHY BE CONCERNED?

The statistics about the collective state of consciousness of our children are frightening. Children around the world are becoming more depressed and lonely as well as more violent. Suicide among children has increased. Stress, aggression, worry, eating disorders, and learning impairments in children are high. These trends are global, transcending culture, society, school, religion, and family. How did it get this way?

Doctors are writing well over half a million prescriptions a year for Prozac-class drugs (selective serotonin reuptake inhibitors) for children.[1] The adult Prozac generation is sending the message to our children that it is all right to numb out to life. How will our children find their vision and feel their dreams if we numb them to what their lives might really be about?

In our efforts to see that our children survive in today's world, we have denied their individuality. We have asked them to do what appears safe rather than what their heart truly desires. Moreover, many have lost hope. We can change this trend!

▶ *The contributors to and the author of this book believe that the way to counter this trend is to recognize, awaken, and activate the dream in every child.*

Are you willing to teach your children to manage their emotions and take control of their own lives with confidence and empowerment?

WHAT IS REQUIRED?

To go against today's social trends is a daunting proposal. The challenge requires our daring and bold response. It calls for a new approach to parenting, mentoring, and befriending our children. Moreover, the responsibility for this parenting revolution lies with individuals—you and me. We are the ones who can change how we treat our *own* children. We are the ones who can push for revision in how we treat *all* children. We can change the course of our experience and our success as parents through new awareness and sensitive action.

To bypass the global trend toward violence and aggression requires our inner peace as well as our passion. Connecting to our inner peace puts us in touch with the dream; this in turn fuels our passion for living, accomplishing, and developing the person we want to be. Likewise, our passion for the dream brings a sense of familiarity and security—the knowledge that we are doing what we need to do and, in most cases, what we *yearn* to do.

How can we help our children find their dream?

1. Watch for and encourage their unique gifts and natural genius.
2. Foster inner peace and harmony.
3. Provide an environment in which the dream can unfold.

REFLECTIONS

Choose a quiet time when you are by yourself to try this exercise. Close your eyes and watch your breathing for a few moments. As you do, notice that your mind quiets and you become aware of your inner feelings. Then ask yourself, "What was my dream as a youth?" Don't attempt to recall it or to scan your history. Just receive what comes. Watch the feelings and thoughts that flow through you. Be aware of them and don't try to hold on to them—just let them pass through. When you feel refreshed, open your eyes and go about your day. You will probably remember aspects of your dream if you haven't done so already. Over the next several days, watch for clues about your dream.

THE EMERGING DREAM

Children offer us clues to their dreams at a very early age through their temperaments, emotional responses, talents, and intelligence. While we will visit each of these topics in depth in chapters 2 and 3, consider the following stories of children whose temperaments later led to their life interests and fulfilling occupations.

Four-year-old Edward asked his parents for cowboy clothes for his birthday. He wore the outfit night and day, avidly playing cowboy games. Within a month, Edward told his parents he was going to be a police officer and asked for police-officer clothes. They were able to find a Halloween outfit that Edward then wore nonstop for the ensuing weeks of police-officer activities. Next Edward asked for a firefighter's hat, since that is what he was going to be when he grew up. Rather than discouraging Edward or becoming impatient with his constant requests, his parents found him the hat, realizing he was living out his repertoire of grown-up roles. He had to dress and act out these roles in order to satisfy his curiosity. This phase ended within six months, by which time Edward had acquired an extensive dress-up wardrobe. As an adult, Edward didn't become a cowboy or a policeman, but he entered a profession in which he studied the minds and emotions of different professionals as a clinical psychologist.

Kimberly, at age two, put back the dress her mother laid out for her each morning and exchanged it for a pair of jeans and a T-shirt. After about a week of these nonverbal clues, she finally told her mother "no" to the dress put out for the day. Blue jeans became the clothing of her choice. Kimberly is now sixteen years of age and still wears her preferred comfortable clothing.

These examples illustrate how each child's unique temperament, with its predispositions and individual preferences, is present from birth. Edward had a natural curiosity about people and professions that his parents encouraged. Kimberly's mother appreciated her daughter's ability to express her preference and encouraged it.

Our children's temperaments show themselves in the way they live each day and how they interact with others. By developing an eye for small clues, matching it with gifts and personal skills we see developing, we build a pathway through which the child's dream can express.

▶ *Each child's unique temperament, with its predisposition and individual preferences, is present from birth.*

NURTURE YOUR CHILD'S GIFT

We can help our children's dreams emerge by using any of the holistic approaches discussed throughout this book. It is through inner peace that the dream unfolds. We use all our parenting skills to discover what is going on inside our children and how that plays out in relationships and events.

Marie was an introverted five-year-old who loved nature walks. She wanted her parents to read only books about trees or other nature-oriented themes. She didn't emulate her mother's cooking or vacuuming. Rather, she modeled working in the garden and watering indoor houseplants. Her parents encouraged this interest by planting a small garden, taking nature walks with an educational bent, and investing in a computer program that identified plants and discussed environmental safeguards. These kinds of activities became Marie's hobbies. Rather than trying to change Marie's shy temperament, her parents helped her develop strengths and interests, knowing these interests would lead her to the next step in her growth.

It takes our parental awareness to watch what *interests* our children. We learn to observe how they play, what they say, and how they adapt to new situations. All of the clues to temperament, emotions, and intelligence are right in front of our eyes. Can we see them clearly?

How Dreams Unfold: Oliver's Story

Some children realize their gifts through their dreams as early as age five or six. More commonly, dreams unfold in puberty and adolescence and give the child a sense of his life mission that he moves toward in an all-consuming way.

Oliver, whom we met in the Prologue, was one whose gift emerged early and stayed in the forefront of his mind in the coming years. This is a common element of an unfolding dream. It doesn't go away. It may take a backseat for a time, but never for very long.

I had a string of dreams with various celebrities popping in and out—until I had one dream about winning an Oscar. I saw myself on stage giving the speech and accepting the award. The next day I found out that my girlfriend had a similar dream. In her dream, she walked into a bar and watched me give my acceptance speech for winning an Oscar on the television over the bar. I had that dream around age fifteen. It was like a reminder of where I was going.

In the span between twelve and eighteen years old, I just knew that I was going to achieve everything that I set out to. I knew I was going to be famous. I knew I was going to have a lot of money. I knew I was going to work with all the people I wanted to work with. This career was set in motion before me, and all this in the process is just learning and waiting. To me the dream is inevitable.

Like Oliver, other children whose dream is alive within them often use the phrase "I know it" or "I can feel it."

▶ *There is no logical way to explain an inner knowing. It is a perceptual, intuitive, and emotional feeling.*

It is not intellectual or logical, and children may not have words to describe it. I asked Oliver to explain what his "knowing" was like:

It is a flash. It starts as a moment—a simple thought that you might normally have. However, the reaction that your entire body and mind have to this thought is different. For instance, there was a time I would think about myself doing a play or a movie, and I couldn't see it. I knew I wanted it, but I could not actually see it and there was no reaction within my body. Then there was one night where I was just lying in bed and it happened. There is a flash of me holding that

Oscar in my hand or being on a set, and my whole body just illumi-
nates. A smile comes to my face immediately. It's euphoric.

The awakened gifts in youth bring such a surge of personal certainty that they have no doubt or question about their journey. It's as if the dream answers those eternal questions, "Who am I? "and "What am I supposed to do?"
▶ *Our children's dreams summon them toward a destiny that can be felt, if not always understood.*

After graduating from high school, Oliver received a full scholarship to study acting. But he yearned to be out in the real world doing it, not studying it.

I've seen the vision and I'm going for it. That is it. Sometimes it's
hard when people tell me that I shouldn't have left school and I
should be making a regular living. "Why don't I just grit my teeth,
bear with it, and make connections?" they suggest. All I know is
that my heart chose another path.

How children's gifts unfold depends on their basic nature and the nurturing they receive. Dreams transcend all religious practices, belief systems, and cultural definitions, although these factors contribute to them and provide a context for them. Gifts need avenues for their expression, as we discuss in the final chapters of this book. Religious and sociocultural aspects can empower or crush them.
▶ *The most important variable that makes a significant difference in how a child's gift reveals itself is how we, as parents, accept, honor, and hold this dream in our own heart.*

How Dreams Unfold: Sarah's Story

Sarah's summer visits to her mother in the New Hampshire White Mountains were normally fun and relaxing times. The summer she was fourteen, however, her mother observed that Sarah was sullen and angry. When they talked, Sarah seemed oblivious to her pervasive, alienating behaviors. Like a swelling stream, something deep in Sarah's unconscious was overrunning the boundaries.

Sarah's anger drove her outside on a hot, humid night when the family was not home. She screamed at the universe, "Why am I here anyway? Who cares?" After a bout of weeping, she returned inside and went to sleep. Sometime in the late night hours, she dreamed her "dolphin dream."

> *I was a small girl, five or six years old, and I was standing on a small pier in a grassy, remote setting. I looked down at the water, which didn't seem normal. Instead, it was an aqua color, translucent and placid. I was captivated with the water, and I could see movement underneath the surface. I recognized dolphins playing. Then they jumped around in the water and called to me, "Come play with us. Come be with us."*

The little dream-girl's fears came up: *I'm not supposed to be here. Mom would get mad. I can't swim without an adult nearby.* As she recited her litany of fears, she ended up in the water. Sarah hooked her arm around the dorsal fin of a dolphin that guided her away from the surface water. She was even more afraid now because they were going deep.

*I couldn't breathe, and I felt lost. Yet there was a calm. A deep inner
voice said, "Go ahead and breathe." So I did. At that point, I felt
everything was all right and I could trust the dolphin.*

*We swam down where the water became darker, and then we
came back up. We resurfaced in a small pool where the water was
thick and gooey like Jell-O. Rocks surrounded the pool like a
ravine, and a gentle waterfall fed the pool. It seemed like a mystical
place to me where time disappeared and my play with the dolphins
was endless. It was a familiar feeling of coming home and feeling
safe and peaceful.*

The last line of Sarah's narrative best sums up the dream
inside each of us.

▶ *When we touch the dream, we feel safe.*

We feel like we are home.

Sarah's insight didn't end there. The dream was Sarah's invitation to set her life direction.

*Right after that dream episode, I had a flood of inspiration. I started
drawing, sketching, and writing poems—more so than I ever had.
I filled sketchpads with dolphins and poetry about what I call my
journeying. The mystery of the event was comfortable, and each
journey I took inside of myself just reinforced the feeling of glee so
that I had to write and draw. Several more dreams followed.*

*In another dream, I was walking along a local beach when I
noticed my mother's friend in the water. It appeared she was drown-
ing, but I wasn't quite sure. I swam out to her to see if she was OK.
I never quite reached her before I saw her at the bottom of the lake*

13

waving to me. I went down to her, and eight dolphins started play-
ing around us. We swam with them for a while.

Then everything disappeared except one dolphin and me.
I asked what my message was. The dolphin replied, "Be with the
dolphins. Be love. Your journey begins."

There were many such journeys. Sarah's dream-dolphins became powerful friends and teachers for her. If she had been in an aboriginal culture, they might have called the dolphin a power animal that came as a teacher. Another parent might have called it an overactive imagination. Sarah's mother recognized that her daughter had found an inner anchor that generated creativity, artistic expression, and a peaceful nature. This gift motivated Sarah to read and learn about dolphins.

► *This is one way we can recognize the dream in our children. It causes them to search. It inspires and motivates them. It becomes a consistent and comforting, yet challenging, given in their lives.*

We can't say no to the blueprint of our gifts without paying the price of dissatisfaction and alienation. Instead, we can recognize dreams as the inspiration that influences our life direction.

I feel that the dream opened a spiritual connection between me and the dolphin that became a guide to me. I turned to the dolphin when I was at a loss to find that same feeling of being secure, like when I could breathe under the water in the first dream.

Through the years, the dolphin connection manifested in my life as a great love for the species. In an altruistic sense, I wanted to help them as well as help other people understand the complexity of their nature. I was inspired to join a swim team the next year.

I wanted to glide through the water like them. Then I became involved in the social activism against tuna canneries and fisheries that fished the dolphins as well. When the tuna canneries admitted their fishing practices, I felt that I was part of a movement that could make a difference. It empowered me.

▶ *Dreams empower children in a positive way.*

James Hillman writes, "[Children] are trying to live two lives at once, the one they were born with, and the one of the place and the people they were born into."[2]

When a child's gift beckons, it may be difficult for those around the child to understand.

I lost faith in my dream just once when I went to college. Family members told me that my dreams were great, but I couldn't survive and pay my bills chasing dolphins. I started reevaluating all of my options, and I came down to the one fact that was real to me. I had a gift, and I wasn't willing to throw it away. I cried most of my first year in college because I wanted my dream.

Just about the time I wanted to give up the whole thing, another door opened again. I met a cognitive psychologist who traveled the world studying whales and dolphins. I changed all of my classes to accommodate my new major, received my bachelor's of science, and will enter a master's program of dolphin research. I'm on my way!

None of us can live without this gift, an aspiration that guides us in the darkest hour. To deny our gifts, to live without a dream is a terrifying prospect. To have nothing that inspires us leaves us like empty clay containers. The essence of who we are evaporates. We would be barren.

OUR DREAM FOR THE FUTURE

In this book, we focus on esteem, empowerment, and wholeness, crucial elements for success in any era. They are even more critical in today's fast-moving, high-tech, crowded, and stressful environments. Perhaps more than at any other time, this era of societal and global interdependence is taxing our energies, depleting our personal resources, and defraying our spiritual development. Too many children and youth feel alienated and alone, without vision or hope. Their dream waits. It may feel dead to them, yet it hovers just out of reach, waiting discovery.

Our children *can* discover their gifts! Join me in starting a parenting revolution. Change the way we think about and treat our children and the way we view our roles as parents and caretakers. Join me in self-education about new applied research and techniques that have been used in education, psychology, medicine, and sports. These tools can help children change for the better under the care of the most influential people in their lives—their parents. Try something new from this book. Give it time and be consistent. Then try another step.

If you care, buy this book for someone else who cares. Pass the word that parenting is about shaping the environment and providing the keys that can facilitate a child's connection to his or her gift.

Together, we'll start a radical new philosophy which knows that love is the key to opening hearts and that in these hearts are the dreams which guide each life. We know that change can happen only through combining our individual efforts. One of us has to start! Join me?

SUMMARY

Our given gift, a dream, is a blueprint that steers the course of our children's lives. Our children's dreams are wrapped like gifts in their unconscious, waiting for parents to open them. Gifts can appear at any age, and we watch for clues in our children's interests, imagination, intuition, temperament, and intelligence.

We want to nurture their gifts and nourish their dream in order to give our children direction, hope, and a purpose they can adhere to throughout life's challenges and busyness. Children with dreams become adults with defined values; they make positive contributions to their community while cultivating an inner peace.

Depending on our parenting style, we can nurture or crush the gift. A positive choice is to accept the dream, honor it, and hold it in our hearts. Dreams usually emerge at the level of knowing or feeling. They are not always logical or easily explained. This is why parents learn to observe their child's behaviors, interests, hobbies, and communication, both verbal and nonverbal.

We can recognize children's unfolding gifts by the motivational factor. Dreams stimulate children and invite them to search or explore further. Dreams inspire children and help them answer the eternal questions "Who am I?" and "What am I supposed to do?"

Esteem, empowerment, and wholeness are path guides to a successful life and to helping children's gifts unfold. They work for all of us, but they are particularly important for children who know their passion. To recognize their gifts and follow their dream, children have to listen to their inner calling more than to outside direction. This takes courage, belief in self, and the ability to follow through and learn from mistakes. *Nurture Your Child's Gift* shows how to uncover those abilities!

2

Managing Emotions

The young man who has not wept is a savage,
And the old man who will not laugh is a fool.

George Santayana

You can't expect to prevent negative feelings altogether. And you can't
expect to experience positive feelings all the time. The Law of Emotional
Choice directs us to acknowledge our feelings but also to refuse to
get stuck in the negative ones.

Greg Anderson

EMOTIONAL INTELLIGENCE

Dreams can emerge when children feel confident and motivated. Optimally, we want children to develop positive emotional expressions in the world and manage any emotional difficulties that challenge them. The emerging research from psychoneuroimmunology has changed the face of parenting by making us aware of the intricate link between the mind and body chemistry.

▶ *This link between mind and body is emotions.*

Emotions have a far greater impact in our actions and thoughts than we previously imagined. Recent studies show that our emotional aptitudes rather than our intelligence quotient may constitute 80 percent of our success in the world.[1]

▶ *A good emotional aptitude is the ability to manage our emotions.*

Well-documented research indicates that we can change those emotional responses which no longer serve us or which constrict our happiness. Altering our biochemistry can change traumas and hurts that impinge on our emotional stability.

For example, a mother and her nine-month-old son, Jason, were hit broadside in their automobile. For several months after, Jason would wake up from naptime as well as in the middle of the night screaming and shaking. Jason's mother believes that he was remembering the accident trauma in his sleep.

The emotion was fearful, and Jason's mother handled it in a loving way. When he woke up crying, she rocked Jason while holding his shaking body. In the background, she played soothing music for his nerves. She also breathed a deep breath while holding him closely to her abdomen and chest. Eventually the breath and music relaxed Jason. His breath slowed enough to match hers, and he would return to sleep. Jason is now a happy and well-adjusted eighteen-month-old, and his mother believes that through her patience, the nightmare memory of the accident is over. Jason won't have the trauma of the accident imprinted in his nervous system. The bonding, music, and breathwork altered the neurochemistry of that event.

Emotional intelligence, a term coined by Daniel Goleman, describes the relationship between emotions, brain chemistry, happiness, health, and general success. It includes

1. Knowing what we are feeling.
2. Perceiving and understanding what others are feeling.
3. Possessing an ability to alter negative and impulsive emotions.

4. Understanding and acting on what motivates us.

5. Developing successful interpersonal skills.[2]

The *pattern* of emotional intelligence is set at an early age as children mirror how the significant others in their lives express feelings and resolve conflicts. Emotional intelligence *is not fixed* in children until approximately age fifteen when the emotional chemistry of the body reaches maturity. In fact, the biochemistry of emotions can be changed at any age.

There is cause for concern, however, because children's emotional quotients are declining due to social neglect. Childhood is a crucial time for developing emotional acumen. It affects how well children learn and directly impinges on their adult happiness.[3] Particularly in the preschool years, primarily parents, relatives, and siblings influence children's emotional-management skills. Because children soak up emotions as well as information, their feelings reflect the predominant psyche in the family.

REFLECTIONS

Look inward for a moment by closing your eyes or moving to a space where there are no distractions. Focus on the emotional atmosphere of your family as it is now. Answer these questions in as much detail as possible: What words describe the current mood of your family? How do the temperaments of each family member reflect, deflect, or contribute to the family emotion? What can you do to maintain an enjoyable family atmosphere?

THE INFLUENCE OF EMOTIONS

Researchers have mapped the location of some emotions in the body. For example, the essential region of the brain that learns, retains, and acts on a fearful response is the circuit between the thalamus, amygdala, and prefrontal lobe.[4] Specific muscles of the body often hold certain negative emotions.[5]

1. Depression can be felt in the brows and the across the shoulder blades.
2. Anger might be held in the jaws and the back of the neck.
3. The shoulders feel responsibility.
4. Our solar plexus may feel issues around safety or security.
5. Our lower back may register fatigue.

We also feel and hold positive emotions in the body as can be seen in those who stand straight, smile often, breathe deeply, and appear relaxed. A simple technique like imaging can elicit positive emotions and physically relax the heart. Music such as Gregorian chants also has a positive emotional effect.

Evelyn's seven-year-old granddaughter, Teresa, came home from school very upset. Teresa physically looked dejected. Her shoulders slumped, and she looked down at the ground as she walked through the house. She went to her room, closed the door, and said she was going to do her homework.

While Evelyn respected her granddaughter's emotional state, she also knew that she would internalize the feelings. Teresa's coping style was to hold things inside and brood about them. Sometimes she would get depressed for several days and not be able to eat. Evelyn devised a way to help her granddaughter.

First, she played upbeat, happy music in the household. Evelyn knew that rhythm and melody positively affect the central nervous system. Time passed, and Teresa opened her bedroom door. Evelyn took the opportunity to enter, sat on Teresa's bed, and waited.

"I know what you want, Grandma," said Teresa. "You don't want me to be sad."

"A little bit of sad is OK," Evelyn replied. "But when a little bit becomes too much, you get sick and don't eat. I don't want you to feel that bad."

"I know, Grandma. You're right." Teresa giggled. "You're always right."

"So what happened?" asked Evelyn. Teresa shared with Evelyn that she had seen her best friend cheating on a spelling test. She didn't want to tattle to the teacher, but neither could she justify or reconcile the action. Teresa confronted her friend during recess. The friend threatened to dissolve their friendship and made ill-founded accusations against Teresa. Teresa's dilemma was whether to be true to herself or to her friend. Evelyn saw that the situation pained Teresa's heart.

Evelyn couldn't tell her granddaughter what to do. However, she could help Teresa find a quiet place within herself so she could recognize what was of value to her. Teresa lay down on the bed, and Evelyn placed her hand on Teresa's abdomen. They breathed deeply together to relax and change Teresa's stress physiology. After several minutes, Teresa said, "Grandma, it makes me sad to lose my friend, but cheating is wrong."

Evelyn asked, "What are you going to do?"

"I'm not a tattletale, Grandma. But I'm not a cheater either. I don't know what I am going to do."

"That's OK," said Evelyn. "You know where you stand, and that's enough."

RECEPTIVITY AND RELAXATION

Expansive emotions positively influence health and well-being. Negative emotions, especially emotions that are not expressed, adversely affect mental and physical health. The following facts, which go against some of our preconceived notions of child rearing, further demonstrate the way in which emotions influence us.

A report from the National Center for Clinical Infant Programs makes the point that school success is not predicted by a child's fund of facts or a precocious ability to read so much as by emotional and social measures—being self-assured and interested.[6]

Emotion is often a more powerful determinant of our behavior than our brain's logical/rational processes. Advertising research supports this fact by estimating that most of our buying habits are governed by emotions, not logic.

Emotions are learned. We can choose to respond in new ways, break old reaction habits, reeducate pain, and repattern emotions that hinder our joy, flow, and creative expression.

▶ *In order to manage emotions, the first, primary, and major step is to learn to relax. The ability to relax is the base factor to reprogramming emotions.*

IS THERE AN EMOTIONAL STATE WE SHOULD AIM FOR?

Positive emotional states support a relaxed and open stance to life and help our children discover and fulfill whatever they dare to dream.

▶ *Expanded emotional states foster esteem and empowerment—two of the building blocks for fulfilling one's life task.*

While we understand that we cannot be eternal optimists, we can foster a positive attitude. Medical research correlates positivism with good health, strong immune systems, success, and favorable interpersonal skills.

We can help our children accept the nature of the real world. For example, things change, and how our children deal with consistent impermanence will clue us in to their ability to persist in using their gifts.

Studies at the Institute of HeartMath in Boulder Creek, California, indicate that five minutes of anger stays in the muscles and organs of your body for six hours. Conversely, five minutes of laughter, humor, and joy also biochemically anchor in your body for six hours. Such a simple statement truly makes you think about how you greet your children each morning. How emotionally open do they go to school in the morning? Are they emotionally invested in cultivating skills to pursue their dream?

An open attitude, acceptance, humor, and joy are certainly the things that we wish for our children and help them develop. And there is an emotional state that we can hold in our minds as the ideal goal for our life—the flow. Just by being mindful of it, we can enter into the flow and practice moving in and out of it. Once the mindbody system understands what flow feels like, it is an easy state to return to.

According to Daniel Goleman, "Flow represents perhaps the ultimate in harnessing the emotions in the service of performance and learning. In flow, the emotions are not just contained

25

and channeled, but positive, energized, and aligned with the task at hand."[7]

Being in the flow, then, implies that you have an emotional goal, a task to focus on. This could be remembering to smile throughout your day. It could be focusing your child in a flow activity—walking the dog, gardening, jogging. Helping your child attend and focus on challenging homework engages flow in persistence and rising to the challenge.

Helping children foster positive and healthy emotions will eventually elongate into flow states. For example, things that enable happiness include good health, positive self-esteem, and feelings of control, optimism, and faith.[8] These qualities also correlate with our active participation in the healing of disease by enabling hope instead of surrendering as a fearful victim to the disease process.

Hope can also be a pragmatic, goal-oriented attitude that a person assumes in the face of difficulty.[9] Hope is an active emotion that can help empower children's dreams.

Successful people have realistic goals and the persistence to achieve them. Happy leaders positively inspire those around them. They have faith—and the ability to make lemonade from sour lemons.

▶ *Relaxing and feeling connected to the flow of life provides avenues for expression of the dream.*

BIOCHEMISTRY OF EMOTIONS

Imagine a time when you were pre-verbal—your body had sensation unlabelled by any linguistic structure. With no words to describe your sensations, you might experience fully the feelings: chills, thrills, tingles, expansiveness, or warmth. If your body cried, you could state the fact " I am crying," with no judgment or emotional label as to what that crying might mean.

Newborn children have no label for sensations. All experience is pure feeling. A hunger triggers a cry for food in human infant and baby bird alike. The feeling is just energy moving through the nervous system and communicating to various organs in the body—just moving energy, no labels! Feelings don't have names and judgments assigned to them—yet.

Children's feelings need to create a pathway in the body in order to be expressed.[10] The more a particular feeling is expressed, the more it becomes imprinted in the mindbody system. Then it becomes an emotion. Feelings are unprogrammed states of sensation.

▶ *Emotions are behavioral responses that have a direction and logic of their own.*

Emotions are learned responses. The good news is that if we don't like our responses to life, we can change them. And there's good reason to do so because relaxed and positive emotions correlate highly with health, longevity, and hearty relationships.

Feelings are our body's communication to the brain. Each person has a set of feelings that could be genetically programmed. There are four basic temperaments or feeling natures that can be observed from birth and define the basic moods which paint our emotional life: timid, bold, upbeat, and melancholy.

Whether the colors of our temperaments are bold, intense, shallow, angry, amused, dark, airy, light, or laughable will depend on our sociocultural programming and our learned responses in specific situations. Temperament is not destiny but the foundation of our emotional patterns.

A group of six-year-old girls was sitting in my living room one afternoon after school watching television. The clink of the ice-cream-truck bell called them to the front door. They stared at the white truck painted with colorful clowns and pondered how to get some of the sweet treats. I observed four emotional reactions from the girls when I refused to foot the bill for the ice cream. My daughter turned away from me with tears in her eyes. I did not support her chosen role of being the heroine. Another young girl sloughed it off and went back to watching television. A third child muttered under her breath about stealing money from her mother's purse for everybody. The fourth child withdrew to the corner of the room and watched to see what the group would do. The girls exhibited one of each response type: humiliation, anger, indifference, and timidity.

My daughter and the child who slunk into the corner both exhibited the shy temperament, but each responded according to her upbringing. The young girl who pondered stealing was impulsive and has exhibited a more aggressive temperament from birth. This serves her well on the soccer field and in competitive events. However, her emotional response when her needs are not met is to try to find a way to get them met without considering the consequences of her actions. This was learned through her acculturation and environment.

Genes play a role in defining basic temperaments—the way we feel about things and our general attitude toward life. In contrast, the intensity, duration, and shape of our responses to life are formed through life experience, interactions, and relationships. These learned patterns are called emotions and comprise the texture and the color of our feelings. Butterflies in the belly may mean fear to one child, tickling and giggling to another, and a strong intuition to another. If we don't like an emotional pattern or find it detrimental or constricting, we can change it.

Research shows us that happiness, joy, going with the flow, and expanded emotional states have the most positive physiological effects. Optimal emotional states are expansive, fluid, harmonious, and creative. In addition, they require relaxed and receptive emotions.

People can learn and maintain emotional coherence when they feel loved, cared for, and appreciated. Those feelings relax and have a calming effect on the body. Heart rate, respiration, and blood pressure synchronize to the relaxed state. Our feeling loved and appreciated can generate relaxation and its physical calming effects.

Love can win! What a powerful implication for the reeducation of our emotions. Simple techniques like music, imagery, breathwork, dance, art, and expressive therapies can enable the body to achieve and maintain a heart-centered state. Medication and cognitive and behavioral therapies may not be the most cost-effective or direct method for maintaining emotional harmony in our children. Instead, teach them to dance. Show them how to breathe life in so fully that they want to achieve their dreams! Try natural means first.

This flow or balanced emotional response is a matter of reeducating our biochemistry. People use food and behavior patterns to reinforce their basic temperaments. We unwittingly engage in activities and eat foods that unbalance our neurochemistry, especially the primary neurotransmitters, serotonin and dopamine. They affect the mindbody and are triggered by our activities and what we eat. Carbohydrates raise our serotonin levels, giving us a sense of well-being. Low levels of serotonin can be responsible for depression, insomnia, and lack of concentration. Dopamine increases alertness, but high levels of dopamine exacerbate this to anxiety, while too little can cause nervous and muscular disorders and even depression.[11]

Food is not the only agent that alters the neurochemistry of emotions. Some forms of exercise, dancing, watching television, playing music, restricted or expansive breathing, meditating, praying, and other similar activities act to reinforce the basic neurochemistry of our emotions and our health. Thoughts, emotions, and physical activity are clearly interrelated. Ultimately, we manage emotions by managing our lifestyles.

SUMMARY

Researchers conclude that as much as 80 percent of our success is related to emotional-management skills. Positive and peaceful emotions ensure that children succeed in life and help them accomplish their life dream.

Goleman popularized the term *emotional intelligence* and defined it as five skill clusters: awareness of our personal feelings, changing negative emotional patterns to positive aptitudes, recognizing and empowering our interests and motivation, developing empathy for others, and negotiating interpersonal relationships.

Early emotional patterns develop in the family nucleus where children first learn emotional-management skills. However, emotional chemistry in the body does not mature until the adolescent years. For this reason, emotional trauma and fixed patterns that don't serve children can change through appropriate parental modeling, interchange, bonding, love, and support.

Researchers have been able to map emotions in the body, since mindbody research shows us that we *learn* emotional responses. Our bodies hold the emotions as specific patterns until we change or re-pattern fearful and constricting responses. As parents, we can help children cultivate the emotional successes required for fulfillment of their dream.

Expansive or positive emotions correlate to good health, well-adjusted attitudes, and feelings of peace and accomplishment. Expansive emotional states foster self-confidence and empowered actions, two of the building blocks of dream fulfillment.

Going with the flow describes an ideal emotional state that allows us to be fluid in life changes and not restricted by fear, anger, or depression. This emotional state of flow allows children to rise up and face life's challenges rather than be daunted by them. Hope is a practical emotion that empowers children's gifts.

Clearly we see that thoughts, emotions, and physical activity are interrelated. The following chapters will help your child establish a lifestyle that supports discovery and fulfillment of their uniqueness

3

Understanding Children's
Temperaments and Intelligence

Every individual has a place to fill.
Victor Hugo

As parents, we readily acknowledge that each child is unique, and it is our greatest desire to understand and work with this uniqueness. In this chapter we look at children through the lenses of intelligence and temperament in order to understand their particular gifts. By fostering children's strengths, we help them develop the confidence and skills that bring forth their dream.

YOUR CHILD'S TEMPERAMENT
We know that each child enters the world with characteristics uniquely his own. We also acknowledge that each child enters with a vision or a dream waiting to unfold.

▶ *Knowing a child's temperament can help us to shape their environment and provide activities to inspire their dream.*

Over the past forty years, research has shown that a child's temperament determines how that child approaches almost every aspect of his or her life. Temperament is genetically based and refers to how we behave. It unfolds through a child's emotions and personality over time. For example, a colicky infant may be a sensitive toddler who develops food allergies. A curious infant who cries often for attention may need to be held and touched more as he grows up. Soothing music might help calm this child. Rubbing hands and toes may offer solace.

The child who doesn't like to be touched may demand to explore, crawl, and not be confined as he grows up. Parents will need to define structure and boundaries for this child. Parents might teach a nervous child to breathe deeply early on to avoid anxiety-producing activities. Shy or timid children may find creative expression an outlet for thoughts and inspirations that they don't share with their parents. A dreamy child might also need physical exercise for grounding, or movement and dance to feel comfortable with the body.

PARENTS HAVE TEMPERAMENTS TOO

About 20 percent of a child's temperament is inherited from parents. In most cases, parents and children with overlapping temperaments get on well and are mutually sympathetic. But if the similarity is an extreme temperament such as a tendency toward hysterical overreaction, the similarity then can cause friction between parent and child.[1]

Our initial feelings and responses to the world are determined, in part, by our temperaments that are one aspect of our genetic and emotional inheritance at birth. In one study, researchers who observed and followed infants' behaviors found that 40 percent of infants were uninhibited and confident, whereas 20 percent were fearful and introverted. However, by age five, only one-fifth of the children in each group still had the same temperament as in infancy.[2] This implies that we do enter this world with set characteristics, yet only 20 percent of us maintain those characteristics completely. The reason is that our culture and environment play a very important role for 80 percent of any given group not to be limited to or by the genetic inheritance.

It is possible that uninhibited and inhibited infants exhibit different neurochemistry in the area of the brain that determines emotional responses and that they differ in the physical response of their sympathetic nervous systems. Some of the physical reactions of inhibited infants include increased heart rate and other physical reactions associated with fear, such as elevated blood pressure and dilated pupils. A few weeks prior to birth, the fetal heartbeat predicts how inhibited or uninhibited a child will be at four months.[3]

It appears that temperament originates in the genetic inheritance. Our parenting styles, our cultures, and our relationships to the world shape the emotional responses. We can infer that children who are consistently inhibited during the early years are at a high risk of developing anxiety, phobias, panic, and obsessive-compulsive disorders. Children who are consistently more responsive show little fear and high excitement. Raised in an environment with few controls or with higher provocations to violence, these uninhibited children have a higher risk of delinquency and violence.[4] The impact of culture and environment on children is at least as important as genetics for 80 percent of any given population.

PARENTS MATTER, NOW MORE THAN EVER

These five reality checks from Dr. James Cameron can help you open your mind and stay attuned to the unfolding temperaments of your children:

1. Knowing their child's temperament helps parents see when to be firm, when to be supportive.
2. Parents who see clearly their child's temperament are better equipped to teach that child how to manage his/her own temperament, building self-confidence.
3. Temperament-savvy parents keep expectations more realistic.
4. Children with different temperaments treat parents differently. Knowing how to respond to these differences helps parents treat each child fairly.
5. Temperament-awareness programs are tools to help parents become the expert in understanding their unique child.[5]

Knowing that we want to develop relaxed, emotionally capable children, as described in chapter 2, take a look at the mindbody techniques mentioned throughout this book to see how you might tailor your child-rearing techniques for your child's temperament.

REFLECTIONS

During a quiet moment, reflect on your child's temperament. How is your child unique? How is he different from other children? What characteristics do you like best?

What attributes would you like to improve?
Does this temperament reflect yours in any
way? How do your temperament styles interact?
Is there anything you would like to change
regarding the interacting temperaments?

Richard was a colicky and nervous baby who became an uncontrollable and aggressive toddler. He was even expelled from preschool because of his behavior. His actions directly affected his ability to develop positive relationships with others. Nobody wanted to play with Richard! Richard's parents were at a loss as to how to influence his behavior. A perceptive school psychologist helped the parents developed some structuring and behavioral techniques to help Richard modify his behavior in an acceptable fashion. Through role-playing, his parents showed Richard how his actions appeared to others. He listened to his words on a tape recorder, and he watched his classroom interactions on videotape. Although Richard was defensive, he made a healthy choice to change his behavior. He saw that other children's responses to him did not feel good inside.

His parents taught Richard some simple but critical social skills he was lacking. Over time, Richard's new behavior allowed him to develop positive relationships with his teachers and peers. Consequently, he became happier and more secure both at home and at school.

During the next year, Richard's parents announced they were getting a divorce. Like most children, Richard believed he was to blame. His response is a common one. Younger children see themselves as the center of their universe. The world revolves around them and because of them. From ages two to six—which Swiss psychologist Jean Piaget called the pre-operational period—children believe concurrent events cause one another.

Richard thought he must be a "bad person," believing he might have said or done something at the time of his parents' separation to cause it. True to his birth temperament, he acted out again, misbehaving and alienating those around him.

▶ *Support and education can retrain basic emotional responses.*

Again, his self-esteem suffered as he slipped into old behavior patterns. What was Richard's heart trying to say to his parents? What awareness was he trying to discern within his own character?

Richard had relearned social skills at an early age, and he will learn new skills to cope with the divorce. What Richard's parents learned is that in times of crisis, Richard may not feel safe and he may act out. If we can observe these types of patterns in our children, we'll be prepared for those instances when they need coaching to work through their temperamental response to a current life crisis.

Deanna and Stan interact and communicate with their son, John, to help instill a healthy self-esteem. Deanna explains that essential to her parenting is respect for the uniqueness of the needs and temperaments of each of her children. For instance, for the first three years of his life, John did nothing but graze on food. Instead of pushing him to clean his plate, she respected his instincts and found that when his body craved vegetables, he would eat them. She continued:

When John becomes irrationally angry or upset because he is hungry or tired, I will hold him and gently explain that he needs to eat or sleep and that is why he feels so overwhelmed. I simply provide him with this information and offer to help, and together we decide what needs to be done. Usually he makes the wise decision because he trusts that I tell him the truth.

I don't view my children as property to be controlled but as individuals needing my flexibility. It is not fair to attempt to mold children to a set style of parenting. What works with one child may not work at all with another. For instance, John's three-year-old sister is strong-willed and much less trusting than John. She needs to feel in control over situations, so I need to empower her more. Consequently, I also need to offer her a lot more structure to ensure the successful result.

My love for my children is unconditional, and I tell them so. Of course, I discipline appropriately, but I always let them know that even when they do something wrong I still love them.

Finally, I believe in myself, and I'm not afraid to make mistakes! It is the only way to learn. If I make a rule for my children to follow and it doesn't work, I'm not afraid to change it. They know I'm not perfect and that it is OK. The respect we have for each other is the key to building a foundation of confidence and trust in our family.

Deanna's words speak to the heart of the parenting revolution: "*I don't view my children as property to be controlled but as individuals needing my flexibility.... I believe in myself, and I'm not afraid to make mistakes!*" As we are, so will be the children.

STRATEGIES FOR HANDLING TEMPERAMENT ISSUES

Psychologist James Cameron gives the following examples of temperament strategies for typical parent-child situations:

In each situation, the child has a different, unique temperament. Several parenting approaches are provided. Which one would you choose?

As the parent of an intense, slow-to-adapt child, you feel, like Rodney Dangerfield, "I don't get no respect. My child doesn't listen. I tell him what to do . . . he just ignores me." Your options:

A. Don't be a wimp. Get tough. Yell. Shake him if necessary. Threaten him with some punishment if he doesn't comply immediately.

B. Be understanding. Avoid confrontation. You can do yourself what you asked him to do. If you do, maybe next time he'll listen.

C. When you want him to do something he doesn't expect to do, tell him well in advance, even give him two or three reminders. Also tell him the consequences if he doesn't comply. And you follow through.

Parents who choose "A" are likely to escalate into shouting matches, if not tantrums. Those choosing "B" are likely to end up being controlled by their child. Those choosing "C" give their slower adapting child enough time to change expectations before they have to change behaviors, then more time with reminders. The choice between compliance or consequences lets the child feel in control. As a result, after the child tests parent's willingness to follow-

through once or twice, he or she routinely chooses to go along with parent's request.

Your slow-to-warm-up, novelty-sensitive child is going to the hospital next week to remove her tonsils. You think:

A. "Hospitals aren't that bad. Doctors and nurses are kind. It's a routine operation. She needs to learn to handle life's misadventures. I don't need to say anything beforehand."

B. "I need to start talking now about what she can expect. Maybe we should visit the hospital first, at least let her see where she will be."

C. "Novelty and change make her so upset beforehand. I'll protect her. I won't tell her until the last moment that she's going to the hospital. No . . . better yet . . . to get her into the car I'll just tell her that morning we're going to McDonald's."

Parents who choose Option A are likely to generate a balky, frightened child. Option C adds distrust to trauma. Option B may be harder for parents, who have to listen to complaints and endure desensitization trips the week beforehand. However, their child is happier and starts to learn to trust hospitals.[6]

A NEW DEFINITION OF INTELLIGENCE

The traditional definition of intelligence as a fixed, quantified value has been replaced by new theories which portray intelligence as a cluster of talents that include interpersonal skills and innate abilities. The foremost authority, Howard Gardner, has redefined intelligence as the ability to resolve a problem or to create a product that is useful in society. It includes the ability to find or create problems so that the groundwork is set for acquiring new knowledge and practicing new behaviors. Recent studies in cognitive science, psychology, and neuroscience suggest that every person's level of intelligence is actually a number of self-directed talents and skills. This makes our whole journey through life a continuing learning experience and dismisses the notion that what a child is born with or gathers through early life experience is all there is. Learning is lifelong! Gardner proposed eight intelligence clusters:

1. *Verbal-linguistic.* The ability to use words and language.
2. *Logical-mathematical.* The capacity for inductive and deductive thinking/reasoning, the use of numbers, and the recognition of abstract patterns.
3. *Visual-spatial.* The ability to visualize objects and spatial dimensions and create internal images and pictures.
4. *Body-kinesthetic.* The wisdom of the body: the ability to control bodily motion.
5. *Musical-rhythmic.* The ability to recognize tonal patterns and sounds and sensitivity to rhythms and beats.
6. *Interpersonal.* The capacity for person-to-person communication and relationships.
7. *Intrapersonal.* The capacity to use inner states of being, self-reflection, metacognition, and awareness of spiritual realities.
8. *Naturalist.* The ability to use intuition and the possession of perceptive capacity.[7]

How can we use our awareness of these intelligence clusters to support our children's development? First, we can acknowledge that each child will be strong in some areas, weak in others. *This is normal development, not a deficiency in our child.*

Recognize that children will not be strong in every area. Notice, however, that their dream will emerge in those areas of their strengths. Knowing this, we can encourage them in the areas of their gifts while at the same time assisting them in those areas where they are not as strong. For example, a child who loves music but can't spell can easily learn spelling through singing.

We can observe where our children's natural talents lie and toward which activities they gravitate in their play, hobbies, and leisure time. Then we can create a stimulating and varied environment so children have exposure in each of these areas.

It is possible that each person uniquely orders their personal experience according to their logic and different ways of knowing. Our cultures also value different skills and strengths. One way to simplify is to divide multiple intelligences into four ways of knowing: *body, imagination, feelings, and intellect.*[8] Creative Systems theory, the work of Dr. Charles Johnston, offers that these four ways of knowing are developmentally related. Let's examine each of the four cycles of this model.

1. *Somatic-kinesthetic intelligence* orders the earliest experiences in our lives. It predominates during the intrauterine period and early life when touch, taste, and knowing provide the fundamental processing. And we use it throughout our life in the sensory modalities. We might observe this type of intelligence in children who are strong in sports, dance excellently, are well

coordinated, and demonstrate strong motor skills. We also see it in children who use their bodies to move, speak, and express.

2. *Symbolic-imaginal intelligence* is the primary language in a child's magical world of make-believe. This way of knowing provides us with myths, symbol, and metaphor for expressing creatively. The last chapter in this book shows you how to work with children in these first two realms to enable inner expression and give dreams an opportunity to express. We see this intelligence in children who have good imaginations, a flare for drama and storytelling, good language expression, and artistic leanings.

3. *Emotional-moral intelligence* moves into the forefront of our lives during adolescence. This is the time when the inner world of magic gives way to the expression of courage, passion, and searches for the heartfelt. The expressive years between nine and eighteen are crucial in two ways. First, the child's dream is likely to come exploding into the everyday world. Second, these are the primary years to refine emotional-management skills for success. As the dream pours out, we want our children to be able to manage it rather than be divided from it. (See chapter 2 for emotional management.) We see these strengths in children with good intrapersonal and interpersonal skills, appropriate choice making, a sense of personal values, and a sense of justice and compassion.

4. *Rational-material intelligence* is an empowerment (chapter 6) of the dream into the world. It reflects our children's ability to follow the logical steps to achieve their success. To do this, they have to think things through, committing time, energy, and resources to the task at hand. We see this kind of intelligence in children who demonstrate strong linguistic background, a logi-

cal approach to situations, and ability to solve problems. This child expresses well, whether verbally or in writing.

According to Charles Johnston, "These four kinds of intelligence interact at multiple levels . . . [and] these modes define human difference, personality style and learning style. No wonder that we are unique! The critical question is not that we learn how to think, but how to think innovatively, in ways that reveal new options."[9]

SUMMARY

In addition to emotional aptitude, there are two more lenses through which to view our children. These are temperament and intelligence.

Temperament is the behavioral style, usually of genetic predisposition, of each child. However, temperament is not a fixed capacity. Culture, environment, and education shape behavioral style throughout a child's life. Knowing a child's temperament enables parents to coach the appropriate skills for dreaming and succeeding.

Newer theories portray intelligence as a cluster of talents that include interpersonal skills and innate abilities. Howard Gardner has defined eight intelligence clusters: verbal-linguistic; logical-mathematical; visual-spatial; body-kinesthetic; musical-rhythmic; interpersonal; intrapersonal; and naturalist. How can we foster our children's intelligence? All children will have both strengths and weaknesses.

Children's dreams usually emerge in their areas of talent and strength. By observing throughout childhood where children gravitate in their interest and motivation, parents can create dynamic as well as peaceful environments and interactions to encourage dreaming, skill-building, and proactive steps toward achieving goals.

Another way to view our children's intelligence is to watch their natural progression through layers of knowing. Children experience four ways of knowing as they develop. Each cycle of knowing is a foundation for later strengths. The four developmental stages are

1. Somatic-kinesthetic awareness predominates during the early years when the five senses engage life.
2. Symbolic-imaginal aptitude develops as children progress from symbol to language to structure of verbal and artistic development.
3. Emotional-moral discernment develops throughout childhood and adolescence. Children define their values, strengthen their character, and learn how to deal with relationships.
4. The rational-material mind develops in children through their problem-solving skills and ability to approach life with imagination as well as common sense.

Helping children use their gifts requires our persistence in observing their strengths, building their weak areas, and shaping their world for the most successful accomplishment of their life—their dream!

4

Understanding General Childhood Development

Our aspirations are our possibilities.
Robert Browning

Another model which can help us understand our children is that of the somewhat predictable stages of chronological development. Children going through these stages have certain needs, behaviors, experiences, and capabilities that are in common with others at the same stage but that may differ from children of other ages. Each child progresses at her own pace and according to her own temperament. Knowing the generalities of these stages helps us watch for emerging gifts by

1. Observing our children's development
2. Knowing which skills to foster at each stage of growth
3. Avoiding unreasonable expectations for our children

What skills do children seek to master and in what sequence? How can we help them express themselves effectively and creatively at each age?

SKILLS DEVELOPED AT EACH MILESTONE

Birth to Eighteen Months

The most important ability for infants to develop is trust, which they learn through their interaction with parents or other care-givers. If an infant finds his needs met for things like warmth, food, hugging, and stimulation, he develops a feeling of safety and, thus, trust.

▶ *A child's self-concept as a lovable and worthwhile person begins at this tender, vulnerable age.*

Trust is the foundation for all relationships for the rest of his life, and trust affects every area of development: physical, intellectual, social, emotional, and moral.

Parents can help their newborn develop a trust bond by meeting his physical needs and by attending and responding to the baby's communications through sound (cooing, babbling, gurgling, and crying), facial expressions, and body movements.

Eighteen Months to Three Years

The toddler period is a time of intense physical growth accompanied by increased physical activity, especially the capacity to walk, run, climb, and control elimination.

▶ *During this period, the toddler's task is to establish a distinct self that is separate from her parent figures.*

The youngster begins to explore and test her environment. Everything is new, exciting, and waiting to be touched—and tasted! This is when she begins to learn about limits (hot stoves, the use of objects, stairs, streets, and cars). It is also the time when she begins to assert herself and gets emotional easily. Her favorite word is "no!" One of her primary needs is increased control over feeding and toilet habits.

Parents of toddlers are diligent in providing their child with a safe environment while teaching self-control and self-reliance. The toddler needs structure and firmness. The parents must make the decisions, especially regarding areas of physical safety and well-being. Keep the rules simple and few yet steadfast.

Power struggles may develop between parent and child, especially over potty training, eating, and sleeping. If parents remain firm through the crying and temper tantrums, the toddler will leave this stage with a solid relationship with her parents. The toddler will trust the parents to establish boundaries. The toddler will know that her parents love her enough to establish behavioral guidelines.

Three to Seven Years
In the preschool and school years, the child's major task is to develop a sense of reality that is distinct from fantasy.

▶ *He has a strong need to differentiate between what is real and what is imagined.*

One of the child's major concerns is gender difference, including interest in pregnancy and birth. It is a period of high creativity.

During this period, the youngster becomes more independent. Because he is now more comfortable with what he can and cannot do, any behavioral problems become of less concern. Parents do not have to say "no" as often. In addition, we delight in watching the intelligence clusters develop and peek through

49

as our children show interest in specific areas. This is a good time to watch for the emerging dream.

Seven to Ten Years

▶ *The child's task is to develop a sense of values to guide decision-making and interests as well as capabilities that lay the foundation for future decisions.*

The child's needs revolve around skill-oriented activities, tasks, and hobbies. Friendship with peers, especially of the same gender, is important. Competition is heightened, as is preoccupation with performance.

School-age children love to help, so assign child-sized chores. Make sure the job fits the child's capabilities so that the youngster succeeds at the task. We support their independence and enhance their self-esteem while always providing for their safety. If there is a single rule for this stage, it is to talk to and listen to your children.

Ten to Thirteen Years

During this preadolescent stage, youngsters transfer allegiance from parents and family to peers. They look to their peers for what is right and wrong. They begin to identify their personal values and watch their world for both congruence and incongruence. They align themselves with whatever calls to their hearts and intuitions as they explore their values and then shift easily to intellectual and physical pursuits. It is a critical time for finding self-esteem and confidence to pursue their dream. It is also a tender age when the dream can be crushed.

▶ *If there is a single golden rule for parents during this stage, it is "Communicate." Listen to what the preadolescent is saying.*

Thirteen to Eighteen Years

The child has two main tasks during this period: to create a personal identity and to establish independence. The adolescent must establish an identity in relation to society, the opposite gender, ideas, the future, possible vocations, and the universe. The process of becoming independent can create tension with the family over limits, values, responsibilities, friends, and plans for the future.

Peer pressure becomes very important to the young adult during this stage. Conflicts can develop between parent and teenager over how much independence the adolescent can exercise. If parents do not support the teen's need for independence, the adolescent will exercise their freedom in self-defeating ways.

▶ *Now is the time for discussion.*

Let the teenager have some participation in decision-making. Show the youth you care by never criticizing them in front of their peers. Save arguments for important issues.

▶ *Remember that although it may not seem like it at times, parents remain the teenager's primary role model.*

INTELLECT AND LANGUAGE SKILLS

Birth to Two Years

An infant's mental capabilities focus on concrete perceptions and experiences. She is learning how to coordinate her sensory perceptions and movements. Her whole life is based on exploration and expression, and there are no real divisions among these modes of expression. Frequent exposure to a variety of sensations will stimulate her sensory-motor learning and coordination. She is also associating feelings and sensations with the stimulator, whether this is a person or an object in her environment.

Two to Seven Years

Language development begins in utero as the child first sensates sounds and becomes familiar with them. At age two, a massive growth in brain structures occurs. This initiates the beginning of interactive language and the process of using words to regulate behavior. Two-year-olds love to explore sounds and their meanings. They may play with "no, no, no," even chanting the words, as they continue the behavior initiating the "no." However, they do not respond well to verbal input, and their actions must often be physically directed.

By age four-and-a-half, children will change their most objectionable behavior such as biting, running away, or saying "no!" in response to their own or others' verbal input. By age seven, language is the most effective method of influencing children's behavior and can be used either to elicit or manage action.

Six to Ten Years

Children in this age range categorize concepts, sequence words in the right order, and gain understanding of the capacity of language. Vocalizations and speech move from play and exploration to offering the child some modicum of control within his world.

▶ *At each developmental step, the child understands his feelings and sensations as the world responds to him, meeting his physical needs and interacting playfully.*

PARENT-CHILD COMMUNICATION

Younger children speak their thoughts aloud both as a way to play with speech and as a way to develop reasoning. Until approximately age seven, children *talk* in order to *think* with words. They hear themselves say the words aloud in order to respond. The speech of a four- or five-year-old is often a stream-of-consciousness flow of words. Over time, this voice is internalized as their "inner parent" voice.

▶ *Clear, congruent, positive communication from parents can help make a child's internal voice a caring one that will guide them kindly and honestly for the rest of their lives.*

This is why it is so important to be honest and kind in our communications both with our children and with others. If we are not completely honest in our expression, children feel it. If we try to smooth things over, they know it. If we speak in hushed tones, they wonder what's wrong. If we gossip covertly, they feel we are hiding something. If our "I am fine, nothing's wrong" speech doesn't match the frown or the worried look on our face, children feel the lack of congruence. They may become unsure of what we say and choose to not listen, or they may think they understand when they don't. What kind of communication are we modeling for them?

▶ *Active listening is an essential ingredient of true communication and demonstrates interest and respect for our children.*

Active listening works wonders with children who feel disempowered or for those who are getting to know their own feelings. Teacher and parent Ilene Krata relays the following story about how she learned to listen to one of her young students by observing him first.

53

Rufus talked with no expectation of being heard. This was the first thing I noticed. I listened carefully to the things he would mutter to himself and I responded to them. At first, he didn't even notice what I did. I'd repeat what he'd say and then give my response to it. When he began to be able to hear me, the look on his face was pure astonishment. He had been talking with no thought of language as communication. He would mumble, "I'm gonna get me some paints and then I'm gonna paint and paint and paint!" but he would make no movement toward the paints. I'd say, "So Ruff, I heard you say you'd like to do some painting. Here are some paints and paper. Now you can paint and paint and paint."

The first painting he did was an apartment house with many windows, and a door where it needed to be. At the top of the building, instead of a roof, there was a figure with a head and two arms with hands reaching up. I asked him who the figure was, but he said he wasn't finished yet. He then chose black and carefully blacked out the entire painting except for the hands and face, which at this point looked as if it was screaming "Fire." Then he stopped abruptly, pointed to the face and said, "That's me."

"It looks like you got out safely," I said with genuine relief.
"Yes," he said.

Ilene had initially thought that Rufus was a hyperactive, learning-disabled child. When he received positive verbal responses, he learned to slow down and focus. He now talks with purpose and dignity. Ilene concluded, "That was all I hoped to give him. Pride. He embraced it, as all children do if given a chance."

REFLECTIONS

Sit down with paper and pen and give yourself a few moments to clear your mind. Find a calm and quiet space inside. Then write as many responses to each of these questions as you can. When you feel your mind is blank again, move on to the next question.

The unkind things my mother (guardian) said to me were. . . .

The unkind things my father said to me were. . . .

The nicest things they said to me were. . . .

The voice of the past that echoes most frequently in my head says. . . .

Now take the time to re-read what you have written. How much of it sounds like you as a parent now? Keep what you like. Are you willing to change what you don't like right now? How would you change it?

NURTURING PARENTING TIPS

1. *Each of the voices in the child's world becomes part of the child's thinking repertoire, and each has emotional associations and triggers.* Our inner voice builds a bridge between the inner and outer worlds, which allows us to move with intention and conscious thought through life.

The inner and outer worlds have begun to take shape at age two, and the child eagerly explores these worlds, led on by the magic and excitement of discovery. Between ages two and six, discoveries are especially focused on patterning movement, speech, and world perceptions. During this time, children develop the intention to regulate their own behavior. It is the era of exploring personal will through body and muscles. They internalize the speech and the experience.

2. *Whatever we say about or to children from our third- or second-person point of view, the child translates into their first-person point of view.*

I was sitting in a doctor's office not too long ago, and I enjoyed observing three generations of family. The little girl was about thirteen months old. When she went to her mother for a hug, the mother cuddled her and said, "You're such a good girl, such a good girl." When she went to the lap of her grandmother, the woman said, "You're a mean little stinker." While saying this, the grandmother tweaked the little girl's nose. Imagine what the little girl heard and internalized: "You're good. You're mean. You stink." In addition, all of these words were associated with a series of both hugs and painful nose tweaks. This is a perfect example of incongruent communication.

3. *Younger children think in terms of I and me because in their early years they are the center of their worlds.*

4. *All interactions, whether verbal or nonverbal, are first felt by children.* Then they apply their experience and language resources in attempting to fit what they are feeling into a familiar category for expression.

My inner parent voice echoes past opinions of my grandmother, teacher, father, and mother. They expressed loving concern for me, unaware that as a child, I translated every word they said into the underlying *feelings* conveyed by their voice tone, posture, and whispers.

They said, "She eats like a bird."

I translated it into, "I peck at my food. Something's wrong with that."

They said, "The wind will blow her away."

I heard, "I'm too skinny."

They said, "Be good."

I wondered, "Why? Is something wrong with me?"

They said, "She has Aunt Edna's nose."

I translated, "It's big and ugly."

They said, "Be home by 10 P.M."

I heard, "They don't trust me."

Clearly, our well-intended expressions of care and concern shape our children's lives. Children remember these phrases as adults thirty and forty years later because the words and associated emotions have tremendous impact. The real question for us to ask ourselves is how much of that voice did *we* internalize and how much does it influence our behavior as adults? How can we use or change the voices to support our own parenting?

Part Two

Building Blocks for

Nurturing the Dream:

Esteem,

Empowerment,

and Wholeness

5

Esteem: A Parent's Gift

Self-trust is the first secret of success.
Ralph Waldo Emerson

The history of the world is full of men who rose to leadership,
by sheer force of self-confidence, bravery and tenacity.
Mahatma Gandhi

Children require positive regard—self-esteem—to fulfill their dream. Esteem is a strong sense of personal identity. Holding ourselves in esteem means knowing that we are worthwhile and valued in some capacity. Esteem is the fuel children need to ignite their dream, face the challenges, and see it through in their lives.

Think of our children's self-esteem as their perceived value of themselves. It is a combination of self-respect and confidence that affects everything they say and do.

Self-esteem is central to what we make of our lives and to the loyalty we have to developing ourselves and to caring about others, and it is at the heart of what we will achieve in the course of our lifetime.

Esteem is the ability to trust ourselves—something that seems to be a difficult task for today's youth. Children measure their performance and define and model their own actions against the examples set by their parents. As parents, our responsibility has no equal in the human experience.

▶ *People who follow their dreams often are going against society's values and so must believe in themselves when outside approval is missing.*

Building Esteem
John's Story

Deanna and Stan adopted John when he was a small child. Being in the restaurant business, they rearranged their lives to accommodate the important person they had awaited eagerly. They didn't hesitate to bring John to their friendly restaurant during lunch and let him "help out." Sometimes helping meant watching Mom stir the soup or wearing an apron like Dad. Sometimes he sat by the cash register saying hello to the patrons.

John developed respect for his parents' work. He also demonstrated an innate friendliness and a genuine smile at meeting people so early in his life. These social skills made him a natural leader in his first-grade class.

John's teacher described him as a child who followed his own instincts and temperament. This is a common trait for those who recognize their gifts or sense their dream early.

According to the teacher, John did his own thing and was not in competition with anyone. Those around him felt comfortable in his presence. John's self-confidence and easy leadership style are characteristic of a child with high self-esteem.

The Role of Family

Self-esteem evolves through the quality of our relationships with each other. It is born within the family because that is where children decide whether they are lovable and capable people. Of course, individuals outside the family also influence self-esteem. Teachers, coaches, and friends all play important roles at different times during our children's growing years. Yet the role of the family remains the most critical experience of esteem building.

In this book, we speak about many things you can do as a parent to support positive self-regard. The kind of person you are is most strongly conveyed by your presence in your actions and your choice of words to your children.

Within the family, children learn who they are and how they are valued. This is where they internalize methods for coping with life. Parents can make the difference between children's confidence and their lack of assurance, between their success and failure in the game of life, between the empowerment of their gift and its loss.

Molly's Story

Molly was adopted into a middle-class family that had waited eight years to welcome her into their home. When Molly was eighteen months old, her parents found her easily distracted and difficult to manage. When they learned that her motor skills were slow to develop, they suspected some sort of learning problem. Professionals advised Molly's mom, who was home with her throughout the day, that Molly needed to be with people, develop early social skills and boundaries, and practice motor skills as much as possible.

Molly's parents did not wait for the teachers and the occupational therapist to come one or two days a week to help

Molly. They started their own program of taking her to museums, parks, and playgrounds where Molly had to interact with children, solve problems, sit through presentations, climb up and down stairs, play on the slide, and swing on the fitness gym.

Molly needed to establish trust in her own body's ability to coordinate movement. She relied on herself and her parents to reflect whether she was doing this. Molly's parents chose their phrases to her very carefully in order to encourage her:

- ☞ "Try another way to solve it," when she couldn't figure out how to do something.
- ☞ "Breathe deeply until you feel calm," before her temper grew short.
- ☞ "Climb up that slide. I'm right here behind you," to help her feel safe on tasks requiring motor skills.
- ☞ "Here's the way to talk on the phone," when she was learning to speak to her grandmother in another state.
- ☞ "Let's go watch the birds in the park," when they wanted her to learn to concentrate on something. Instead of relying on television, they used everyday activities.

Despite her problems early in life, Molly did well in first grade both socializing and learning to attend to and complete her tasks. She did well because her parents facilitated experiences where she felt successful. Through these small successes she developed confidence in herself.

► *Children formulate their self-image based on what they perceive we think about them.*

Esteem starts in infancy. When our children's physical and emotional needs are met from the beginning, it lets them know we think they are worthwhile and lovable. It establishes a parameter of safety that says, "Explore your world; you are safe."

Beyond infancy, esteem is continually influenced by the messages we send, the behavior we model, and the environment we create. Children formulate their self-image based on what they perceive we think about them. We send our children images directly in both spoken and nonverbal forms, and this communication reflects the qualities we bring to our interactions. For example, take some time to observe how you come across to your children. They may see you

1. In a demeaning manner, so that over time our children perceive that they are no good.
2. In an angry or disapproving manner, implying to our children that they are bad or unworthy.
3. In a genuinely praising manner, so that our children feel we are pleased with them.
4. In a supportive manner, so that our children feel confident in their actions.
5. In an inclusive manner, so that our children feel part of a family team in which there is much to learn from parents, siblings, grandparents, and other extended family members who truly care about them.

REFLECTIONS

Write this phrase on the top of a sheet of paper:
I love my child if. . . . Spend the next several

65

moments in utter honesty with yourself by writing responses to the phrase. You are discovering what conditions you unconsciously place on your love for your child. Your child may interpret this as "I am lovable only when I do. . . ." Once you discover conditional love, write out a brief plan of action about how you might be freer with showing your love to your child.

If we are frequently angry, disapproving, or scolding toward our children, they may believe that we are withdrawing our love from them. This can damage their self-confidence.

On the other hand, when we are consistently supportive, respectful, and patient in dealing with our children, they reflect their positive self-regard back to us. Remember how cheerful and supportive we were when our infant started walking? If we maintain that genuine enthusiasm and delight as our children accomplish new tasks, we will help them develop the esteem necessary for their success.

▶ *Children learn that we can love them as people and still disapprove of their behaviors.*

A child's self-image is far more complex than simply mirroring how others view him, however. While family influence is unquestionable, it is not realistic to place all the responsibility for this important factor of a child's esteem on the family or significant others. The child's temperament and how we handle their temperament, as well as their developing emotions and aptitude, are the filters through which they see themselves.

▶ *Children actively participate in developing their own sense of esteem.*

Children who start out with high self-esteem generally have a higher frustration tolerance, better attention span, and far fewer behavior problems. Children with low self-esteem tend to feel, "I'm not OK, I can't do anything right, nobody likes me." Parents are not directly responsible for children's feelings about themselves. The best we can do is try to be positive models, keep an open mind, and try to learn from our mistakes.

IT'S OUR RESPONSIBILITY

Esteem is about building responsibility for oneself and to the world. Educator and author Lilian Katz offers seven ways in which we can help strengthen our children's self-esteem:

1. *Help them build healthy relationships with peers.*

Seven-year-old Jeremy was complaining that he didn't have any friends. By asking the right questions, his father got him to admit that he may have driven his friends away by being overly bossy or demanding. Together they came up with ways of bringing his friends back. With his father's coaching, Jeremy visualized how his bossiness might feel to others. They role-played an encounter between Jeremy and a friend, with Jeremy as the friend. Once Jeremy empathized with his friend's feelings, he was better able to discuss possible solutions to the problem.

2. *Help them not only build and sustain friendships but also end them when necessary so they learn to assert themselves.*

Six-year-old Sheila had a friend visiting. They were playing quietly in her room when she suddenly ran to her mother in a rage because her friend insisted on playing "teacher" again. "I never get to be the teacher when we play school," Sheila complained. Her mother asked Sheila what she might say to her friend to make the play fairer. After some thought, Sheila came up with the suggestion that they take turns. Allowed to come to her own conclusions, Sheila was able to settle the dispute without overt parental intervention. Instead of refereeing the play, this mother helped her daughter come up with her own rules of play.

3. *Be clear about personal values and keep the lines of communication open about experiences outside the home.*

Gina, a shy and sensitive ten-year-old, witnessed a gang of boys in her neighborhood hang a cat from a tree. When she came home in tears, her sister, who was her guardian, was at work, so there was no one to talk with. Gina became moody and sullen following the event.

When Gina tried to shut the event out of her life by not talking about it, her sister could read the signs of anxiety. The sister asked around the neighborhood and pieced together some of the tale. Rather than dragging the story out of Gina, she devised a plan to motivate Gina out of her depression. Being a nurse, she understood her sister's sensitivity to others' suffering. This sensitivity could be her sister's gift rather than the cause of discomfort.

First, her sister took Gina to a small nursing home one evening and allowed her to help. This delighted Gina and definitely lifted her mood. After talking with her sister, she decided to spend her afternoons after school at the home of an elderly aunt where she could help the aunt with housework and cooking.

Gina's sister used the crisis to develop a successful plan of action. This increased Gina's esteem rather than just talking about what was wrong.

4. *Deepen their sense of self-worth by responding with interest and appreciation to their interests and efforts.*

When Karen married for the second time, her five-year-old daughter became the youngest child among three older stepchildren. Karen was determined to help her daughter develop a hobby or talent so she could build a stronger sense of self-worth. In spite of running the schedules of four children, spouse, and household while also working as a librarian, Karen gladly took on the responsibility of enrolling her daughter in ballet and tap lessons. Several months later, it was gymnastics. After that it was piano.

One day after school, the now-six-year-old daughter answered the doorbell. Her piano teacher started to walk in the door when the daughter planted herself firmly in front of the piano teacher. With as much stature and gruffness as she could muster, she yelled at the woman, "My mommy says I don't have to take your old piano lessons anymore. So go away!" Freed of her obligatory task, the child went outside to play.

The piano teacher called Karen that evening, angry at being dismissed in such a manner. While Karen apologized, she got the message her daughter was sending to her: Stop the lessons already! You haven't heard me!

Typical of a trying-too-hard parent, Karen sat down with her daughter. They reviewed all of the lessons. Karen actively listened to her daughter without trying to solve some problem or giving advice. As Karen put it, "I was great. I changed my whole demeanor. I finally heard my daughter!"

Karen's daughter wanted to paint. She didn't want lessons; she just wanted to paint. They set up an easel, bought art supplies, and picked out picture postcards that the daughter liked to copy. The result was phenomenal. A real talent emerged that developed into a lifelong pursuit.

The child's dream was trying to express. No one was listening. When it burst through the child onto the piano teacher, at last the door opened for real communication. We can appreciate our children's interest. Can we hear them when they communicate their gifts and interests to us?

5. *Engage them in tasks that offer challenge and stretch their abilities to give them a sense of accomplishment.*

When Joseph was eight years old, he met a new speech therapist. His response to this one was as blasé as to all the others he'd worked with since he was three years old and a physician pronounced him a stutterer. The label brought too much attention, worry, and loss of confidence for the child who couldn't talk right. He met over the years with each therapist for the burdensome one hour a week in an office. He tried his best. The results were always the same. He continued to stutter.

The new speech therapist was different. Nineteen years old and fresh out of school, she saw Joseph as a child with a crisis in confidence, not a stutterer. She taught him a behavioral technique of squeezing his thumb before he started to stutter. It took his mind off the stuttering, and he managed to get through words now and then. They practiced frequently, getting ready for a big debut—Joseph would go out in public and practice speaking.

"Where would you like to go on an outing, someplace fun and exciting for you?" the therapist asked Joseph.

"No problem. To the beach, for sure. Do you mean it?" he asked.

"Oh, Joseph, I definitely mean it," the therapist replied. "Let's go someplace exciting and fun for you. You'll be relaxed when you talk to people, and you can practice, OK?"

"You got a deal," Joseph said as he gave the teacher the high-five slap of a deal completed.

That Saturday at the beach actually brought more anxiety for Joseph. Talking about asking for a hot dog and Coke from the vendor was easy to do. But standing in front of the vendor and opening his mouth was traumatic.

Joseph stood before the vendor for a full ten minutes. The therapist knew she could not interrupt the crucial moment of decision-making, even if her stomach was knotted in anxiety for her student.

Standing behind Joseph, she watched him practice the hand maneuver behind his back. Five times. Ten times. Fifteen times. Then he did it! He took the first step forward! Finally, he kept moving.

He approached the vendor with his dollar bills in one hand. The other hand moved behind his back. He asked once, "I, I." He stopped and took a deep breath. He tried again. "I'd like a hot dog."

He did it. A brief request without hesitation. Joseph didn't wait for his hot dog. He turned and ran to his speech therapist. He laughed. She cried. They hugged. He jumped several twirls in the air and landed on his back in the sand. Joseph found his confidence.

He faced the impossible. With help, he stretched to meet the challenge, because feeling bad about himself and stuttering the rest of his life was a worse dilemma. It took only one moment to feel good again, and it lasted for the rest of his life.

6. *Treat them with respect, ask their views, take their opinions seriously, and give meaningful feedback.*

Jason's family had been farmers for generations. He had a deep love of nature and animals. He wanted the same for his children. After his wife died of cancer, he returned to the family farm with his seven-year-old son and four-year-old daughter.

To help his children develop the same appreciation for life that he had, he asked each child to help him raise a litter of piglets. Excited and happy to do so, the children seemed to develop a personal relationship with the animals as time passed.

All along Jason explained to the children the process of feeding the animals and fattening them for market. He reviewed with them what the steps were to market and how the animals provided pork chops for their supper and the bacon at breakfast.

Finally, the time came to slaughter the pigs for meat. While the children did not accompany Jason, they assured him that they were fine with the events.

The next morning, Jason's son announced, "I'm not going to eat meat. I am going to be a vegetarian."

"Why?" Jason asked.

The answer Jason received surprised him. His son lectured him on the slaughtering practices, the fear the animals felt, and so on. His son opened files on the computer showing facts to support what he was saying. His son's behavior reminded Jason of a college professor lecturing young students.

His son had studied the subject in his spare time throughout the year. While the child understood Jason's position, he also developed his own position, modeled after his father's steadfastness to his principles.

Jason respected his son's choice. The household accommodated his food preferences because of the time and earnest effort the child had put into this subject. Jason's son earned the nickname of "the little professor."

Again, the dream inside the child was silently emerging, helping him to explore and fortify his personal beliefs at such a young age. Jason's son grew into an educational researcher and social activist, teaching adolescents about careers in the field, including farming and animal husbandry.

7. *Help them cope with defeats by letting them know that your love and support remain unchanged.*

When Lelani first started school at age six, her classroom teacher recommended her for the gifted program, and the school psychologist confirmed this. Lelani skipped first grade and entered a gifted classroom for third graders. She was stimulated intellectually and participated in scholastic competitions, building computers, writing music, and other similar activities.

When Lelani was fourteen, her mother died. Lelani went to live with her father and his family after her mother's passing. She was excited and frightened.

Lelani told her father that she was willing to attend the large public high school. She was scared to death, but she didn't want to be a burden to her father.

When she enrolled at the public high school, they refused to put her in any gifted classes. Instead, the guidance counselor put her in developmental classes because everything else was filled. "OK," she said to herself. "I am going to make this work."

In the first month, the developmental English class was boring for her. She did the assignments and received average grades. She didn't put in all of her effort because she didn't want to stand out. During the second month of school, things got worse. After an English examination, the teacher took all of the tests and threw them in the trash. She lectured the students that after grading half of the class papers, it was obvious that all of them were failing her class. Therefore, she was going to give everyone an F on this test.

For sensitive Lelani, this was unfair. She stood up in class and asked the teacher to pull her paper out of the trash and grade it. The teacher refused, threatening to reinforce the F a second time if Lelani continued to interrupt her lecture.

Lelani burst into tears and ran from the room. She had never encountered such a teacher or situation. The next weeks the teacher became even harder on the class. Lectures became curt. Homework assignments were longer. Lelani easily accomplished all of the tasks, but this didn't please the teacher. Instead she berated Lelani in front of the other students. Lelani gave up.

One evening she became nauseated and was unable to eat. She cried at the dinner table and went to her room. Her father had been aware of her mounting tension, but he had chalked it up to all of the new adjustments. This evening he followed her to her room.

"Lelani, what in heaven's name is wrong?" he asked. She looked at his face and saw genuine concern.

"I've just failed," she replied. "I've tried to make school work, and I am utterly defeated. I just want to curl up and die."

"You have rarely failed at anything, Lelani. This must be devastating. Please tell me what happened."

As the story unfolded, the father's concern turned to anger. His first response was to pull Lelani out of public school and place her in a private school. In truth, that would have made her feel safer and more confident. However, Lelani's gut-level feeling was that she needed to stick out the experience of public school.

Lelani and her father together decided on a plan of action. Within a month of this incident, the teacher quit due to poor health. Lelani applied for a different set of classes, determined to let her talents surface in this environment. She ended up having a great year, and it took faith on her father's part to let her stay in the public school.

Lelani's intuition told her to build her confidence again and not to let the system beat her down. It was the hardest decision she'd made. Moreover, her father honored his daughter's perseverance in the face of peer ridicule and defeat.

EARNED SELF-CONFIDENCE

Self-esteem programs have been criticized for handing out praise indiscriminately. Some studies suggest that if self-esteem is not earned, it is worthless. There are elements of truth to this argument. On one hand, it is a child's right to feel loved, respected, and intrinsically valued. Offering these is part of our parenting role. On the other hand, indiscriminate and insincere praise has no educational value.

It is important to find the balance point. Love and respect for our children can be a constant in their environment. If we want them to feel truly good about themselves, we can help them build self-confidence from within.

▶ *Self-esteem comes from mastering skills that lead to growing confidence.*

As parents, we can foster a positive self-concept by encouraging our children to

1. Use their talents and abilities.
2. Master hobbies or skills.
3. Manage their emotions.
4. Persevere at a task.
5. Accomplish a goal.
6. Complete a hard assignment.
7. Follow through on a project.

All of these help children build intrinsic value when we express appreciation of them. And here is the twist!

▶ *Our children can complete many tasks, but they need someone to value their efforts in the early years before they know that these tasks have intrinsic value.*

Although praise and encouragement are important, we must be careful not to set our children up for failure by our enthusiasm. Balance is the key, based on awareness and discernment.

THE POWER OF AFFIRMATIONS

We want to give our children lifelong skills and tools to accomplish their dream. To believe in themselves. To use their gifts. We want to see them succeed at what they love—it is at the heart of our parenting role.

Affirmations can help. They have the effect of "changing the subject" of a child's outlook from what might be a negative, fearful, or defeated focus to a positive, loving, and confident one.

▶ *Affirmations help children create a positive and affirming inner voice— one they will have with them all of their lives.*

In our daily conversations with children, we can use positive affirmation to express confidence in their abilities. Teach and model how they can use affirming thoughts and words for themselves and with others.

When using affirmations with preschool children, it is best to keep the affirmations worded simply with a positive intent: "I can do it" and "I am special" and "I am loved." Being special and loved are ends in themselves. We can also expand the meaning by elaborating about why they are special: "Because I can write my name" or "Because I'm part of a loving family."

Once children reach their elementary school years, they can use affirmations in more active ways such as writing them, recording them into a tape player, creating diaries, or drawing pictures or symbols for their affirmations. Chapter 9 provides more information on how to use affirmations.

RELATIONSHIPS WITH OTHERS

Parents and other adults who are important to children play a major role in laying a solid foundation for esteem. Before our children ever build relationships with others, they build them with us.

Part of our role is to teach and model respect, fairness, and empathy. To do this, we can create an environment based on these principles. We can establish firm limits that ensure our children's actions don't harm them or those around them. We can teach them to treat others with kindness and respect. By living our parenting roles with kindness and respect, we give our children opportunities to develop the same.

▶ *One principle we want to teach our children is that while they are truly important, they are no more so than any other family member.*

Parents can help children see themselves as others see them. Because we have more experience with interpersonal relations than our children do, we can help them understand the nature of friendship. By observing them at play with friends, we can learn much about how they interact with others. When we see behavior that runs counter to developing friendships, we can point this out in a positive, constructive manner. We can assist our children not only in helping them to build and sustain friendships but also to end them when necessary.

Sarah overheard her daughter, Kerry, giving in to a friend's demands repeatedly. One of these demands involved Kerry watching her friend steal money from her mother's purse. Kerry started having stomachaches.

Sarah discussed with Kerry what friends are really like. They read several books about the value of friendship. Sarah encouraged Kerry to understand that friends don't get each other in trouble, and they don't steal.

Kerry decided she would really like to say something to her friend or even break off the friendship, but she feared confrontation. Sarah played an encounter between Kerry and her friend, allowing Kerry to play both roles. She asked Kerry how she felt when her friend made so many demands on her. What would Kerry like to say? Together, they came up with some assertive visualizations and affirmations. Sarah role-played the encounters again and again until her daughter was confident of herself and felt equipped to stand up to her friend.

Building self-esteem is really very simple. How would you feel if you were your child? The words you use, the actions you take, the faces you make—are these things that you would say to yourself?

6

Empowerment: A Gift from Within

To accomplish great things, we must not only act, but also dream,
Not only plan, but also believe.

Anatole France

Self-esteem is the first step toward achieving the dream; empowerment is the second. Empowerment is an individual's ability to think through options and act on his beliefs.

Much like esteem, we model empowerment for children by how we speak, value, discipline, and teach. Empowerment includes learning about

- Possibilities and choices
- Actions and consequences
- Options and priorities

▶ *Empowerment is the individual's ability to think through options and take action.*

Empowerment, then, is

- An attitude
- A belief in the self

☞ An ability to sustain positive action toward a personal goal

☞ An inner knowing

☞ A willingness to take risks

Through empowerment, children can create meaning in their lives. Remember what it was like when you accomplished something through your own effort and persistence? It was from your inner drive and exertion of will. This is empowerment—finding the dream, the motivation, and the action!

As much as we would like to, we cannot give empowerment to our children. Each person must empower himself or herself. It is uniquely a gift from within. Yet when we consciously foster compassion, spontaneity, humor, and strength, our children respond. These positive qualities infect others with the same zeal. This is how we can empower another person.

No matter how hard we try, the most we can do as parents, teachers, and friends is empower ourselves. By doing this we will actively encourage that strength in our children. We can also create an environment that leads to empowerment.

QUALITIES OF EMPOWERMENT

Empowered people demonstrate certain habits and actions:

☞ They think for themselves.

☞ They understand the longer-term consequences of their actions.

☞ They feel good about themselves.

☞ They have a cheerful smile or kind act for others.

For our empowered children, we want them to

↷ Relate well with others

↷ Trust their actions and thoughts

↷ Adapt in learning new skills to meet changing situations

↷ Acknowledge and move through defensive behaviors of anger, depression, blame, and woundedness

↷ Develop a level of self-discipline that springs from a trust in their intuition

↷ Greet the day with a feeling of self-confidence and a positive expectation of what life has to offer

↷ Use humor and laugh often

↷ Creatively overlap work and play

↷ Accept personal strengths as well as weaknesses and be forgiving toward themselves and others

↷ Accept and give love

REFLECTIONS

Relax and breathe deeply. Then imagine an intense and happy moment when you felt confident, with a strong belief in yourself. Can you sense a moment of empowerment? Re-create that experience. Where are you? What were you doing? Who was with you? Why did you feel so relaxed and confident? Try to recall what you were thinking and feeling at that time. Sense the feeling of empowerment in yourself. Perhaps you will feel a strengthening in your body. Can you re-create that sense of empowerment in your life now?

Affirm: I sense my own health and gift of empowerment.

TRANSFERRING POWER

What can empowerment possibly mean to a child who not only feels powerless—but who also *is* powerless in so many situations? We make all the decisions for our children when they are young. We start with choosing their foods, activities, clothes, bedtimes, and schools. Later, we influence their choice of friends, games, and rules that we expect them to follow. We do this because we love them and realize they need rules and structure to feel safe. Then, what exactly does it mean to foster self-empowerment in our children?

▶ *The process is actually a transference of power, in which children eventually model and learn the same abilities to function plus a belief in their own unlimited gifts.*

Children eventually model and learn the same abilities to function, sensing their life paths and gaining the confidence and ability to walk them. Remember that sense of unlimited potential we felt when we first looked at our tiny babies? Every parent has experienced it, a moment of such deep and unlimited love.

▶ *The power of our belief in a child's limitless potential is the key ingredient in fostering healthy self-esteem and empowerment.*

Supporting our children's empowerment requires that we trust and respect their unique temperaments, aptitudes, and emotions. Empowerment demands our interaction! We help children to empowerment when we

- ☞ Help them think through their choices and options
- ☞ Step back while they make their own decisions
- ☞ Trust their wholeness to guide the way

Whether we agree or not with their final choice, we respect them and trust that our seeds of empowerment are sprouting. This is not always easy, especially in the adolescent years. If we honor their uniqueness, we increasingly must realize that we don't always know what is right for them. As they mature, we allow them to choose their own paths. Their heart has the dream, and it will emerge.

▶ *The process, then, is to rear our children for their fullest potential by gradually transferring our belief in their empowerment and unlimited potential to them.*

There is a definite connection between empowered adults and certain qualities in childhood. What are some of the qualities that we can foster and nurture right now?

A Sense of Humor
A sense of humor is the ability to see things that are funny, out of the ordinary, or that don't necessarily go together. A sense of humor is one of the first qualities we want to see in our children. They can laugh when you change the order of the normal routine and give them dessert first, laugh in delight when they play dress-up, or think it's funny when they "read" to you rather than the other way around.

Encouraging Laughter

We can encourage children's laughter and help them to identify that personal quality by simply saying things like

- ☞ "Gee, you have a good sense of humor."
- ☞ "I like the way you laugh at things."
- ☞ "I like the way you can see both sides of the coin."
- ☞ "I'm glad you don't take life so seriously."

When Jason was four years old, his seven-year-old brother wanted to ride the Magic Mountain roller coaster at Disney World. To ensure their safety, the parents sat in the seat behind them. At the first dip into a steep downhill plunge, Jason was near tears. He turned in his seat and looked to his mother for consolation. This is what she reported:

> *When Jason turned to me, I was in the midst of trying not to regurgitate my lunch. I am sure that I was as pale as a ghost was. In that moment of seeing my child's face, I realized that I had to laugh and whoop it up. If I did not he would never ride another roller coaster. I smiled through my own terror. He looked at me hard. Then he imitated my grin. I smiled even wider and laughed aloud. Stricken Jason did the same. After a moment or two, he was actually laughing and having a good time.*

Acknowledging Feelings

▶ *Children who learn empowerment are spontaneous and open to new people and experiences, but with discernment.*

Children can discern when it is safe to be open and when it is best to move away. They are trustworthy individuals. To foster these qualities, we can encourage our children to move through their fears rather than letting fears freeze them into inaction.

When we are dealing with children's fears and other feelings, it is important to forget the classical words that many of us learned, words like *accepting, process, clarifying,* and *venting.* Instead, there are two words to keep in the forefront of our minds: *recognize* and *respect.*

- ☞ Acknowledging feelings means *recognize* and *respect.*
- ☞ Recognize the feelings that the child is experiencing. This validates the experience without sympathizing, correcting, or judging it as inappropriate.
- ☞ Respect the feelings as genuine.

Recognizing a feeling authenticates the experience without sympathizing, correcting, or judging it as inappropriate. Children have overwhelming and fluctuating feelings that change day-to-day, group-to-group, and parent-to-parent. Children's sensitive natures can go into overload quite easily. In this book, look for techniques, especially breathwork and music, that can help stabilize feelings. They are described in chapters 10 and 11.

Living with Joy

Children on the road to empowerment enjoy themselves in most situations. They have a sense that life is fun, not something to be feared or dominated. They will share easily because they have no fear that things will be taken away if they give up control. Sharing without being a "chump" shows a sense of give-and-take that becomes a strong sense of self as an adult. Often the children who find it hard to share will find it difficult to generate multiple options in their own thinking as adults.

Honoring Empowering Moments

Actively teach your child to honor the moments of empowerment. When we are talking about something that our children have just done well, we can simply say, "Think of this moment of success in your mind. I want you to appreciate yourself." Alternatively, "See yourself doing just what you did when you were successful. Affirm 'I did it well.'" This will teach children how to build on their successful moments.

Personal Qualities

We all have characteristics that are strong and confident and others that we perceive as weaker. Helping our children recognize and develop a balanced picture of themselves assists them to make healthy choices. In child development, most specialists agree that strengthening children's talents develops empowerment.

Honoring Strengths

Identifying areas of strength helps children develop confidence. Try this: Suggest that your children develop a list of their positive personal qualities. These may be

- ☞ A warm sense of humor
- ☞ A strong ability to create with their hands
- ☞ Helpfulness to others
- ☞ Courage in difficult situations
- ☞ Recognizing fear and moving through it anyway

Next, suggest that your children make a list of the positive personal qualities of each family member. This encourages children to look for and name the positive qualities they see in others. By doing this, they feel connected with others.

Bob, a second grader, was shy and afraid of attending a new school after the family's relocation. Working together, Bob and his teacher made lists of their positive qualities and drew pictures to accompany them. He showed himself as being strong and able to carry things for his mom.

Then Bob agreed to participate in a small skit put on for the kindergarten classes. His part was to stand up with three other children and carry a sign depicting a butterfly. On cue, he was to lift up the sign for all to see.

At first Bob was reluctant to face the class. During practice, his teacher actively encouraged him, expressing her confidence in his ability. She gave him concrete guidance: "Turn around. It is OK. You can carry the sign and hide at the same time if you want."

After his first performance, he suddenly felt safe carrying his sign any way he wanted. In the next three kindergarten performances, he progressively moved forward, raising his sign so he could be seen. He became animated in his actions, singing increasingly loudly. Much to everyone's surprise, by the end of the year, this same boy volunteered for the all-school talent show.

REFLECTIONS

Take a few moments to reflect on the good qualities you perceive in each of your children. Also, reflect on the qualities that you believe you exhibit as empowerment. Jot down a few of these "plus" qualities for each member of your family. The very act of making a list is, in and of itself, empowering. Encourage your whole family to look for strengths in each other.

Affirm: We build upon our strengths to support empowerment.

IDENTIFYING AREAS OF GROWTH

We all have qualities that are weaker than others. Usually, these areas have to do with fears. By sharing with our children some of our own mistakes, fears, and growth areas, we can gently coach them into paying attention to those areas they want to improve.

▶ *Areas of growth are opportunities for learning!*

By using the term *growth areas* instead of strengths and weaknesses, we focus on expansion. It is important to create a balanced picture. We can do it simply by saying things like

- ☞ "You and I are a lot alike; we both get impatient and want things done right away. That's something we need to work on—being more patient."
- ☞ "I'm not keeping my mind on what I am supposed to do today. Does that ever happen to you?"
- ☞ "I saw you take a deep breath before getting angry. That was great."
- ☞ "Why don't you put on some music and dance off your excess energy?"

REFLECTIONS

Spend a few moments focusing on areas in which both you and your family members may need to develop skills and attitudes that will lead to fuller empowerment. What are the areas of growth that are needed? How can you help foster them in your family?

Affirm: Areas of growth are challenges that can be met.

FEAR AND SAFETY

Empowered children feel safe in their world. They don't approach life from a place of fear and restriction. They reach out to life in an open and loving way. In relating to others, they know to trust their intuition as to when it is advisable to be open and when it is not.

Since children's initial learning comes through interactions with parents, let's be honest and evaluate our own attitudes toward the world. Difficult as it may be, let us have the courage to ask ourselves the hard questions about how we view the world. Here is how some parents responded to some self-appraisal questions. Why don't you write down your answers, too?

What do we see about our speech that we would like to change?

1. "Every time my daughter asked me my opinion, I would say to her, 'What do *you* think?' She finally got very angry that I wouldn't give her any guidelines. I quit copping out on being honest with her."

2. "My son was a daydreamer and dawdler at meals. Every time we sat down to a meal, I would automatically say to him, 'You better eat now or I'm gonna whip ya.' When my wife counted that I had said that phrase ten times in one hour, I was embarrassed. I guess I needed to look at how I was talking to my kid."

3. "One morning I woke up to the sound of my three-year-old daughter's voice. She was talking to someone very sternly. 'You be good now or you're going to that corner.' I sneaked out of bed and down the hallway. That little imp had her hand on her hip, sashaying back and forth in front of our poodle. My God, she sounded just like me. Better yet, the dog was really trying to understand. He sat patiently, following her every move."

What makes us feel not safe in our world? And do I convey this fear to my child?

1. "We live in New York City, and I hate crossing the busy Manhattan streets. When my daughter is with me, I do convey my fear to her. I grab her arm tightly and practically drag her across the street running. My gosh, she's ten years old. I guess she is able to cross the street alone, isn't she?"

2. "I am afraid of peeping toms. When I go to bed at night, I close all the blinds in the house, including my son's room. When I get up in the morning, the shade in my son's bedroom is always open. I always yell at him, but he doesn't listen. He says he likes to look at the stars."

3. "I lost my first child to SIDS. I don't want to lose my second child. I am extremely protective of her activities and playtime. I am always with her. That is how much I cherish her."

Each of these examples regarding fear shows how we as parents might project on our children what we find fearful in life. Yet these things may not bother our children at all. What we can focus on instead is feeling safe. Empowerment has a great deal to do with feeling safe and connected to others.

Children are vulnerable to anger, rage, and punishment, and most of the time, they haven't a clue about when or why these things occur. They may feel powerless and fearful in the presence of intense emotion and may respond with anger or violence.

▶ *Many parents are committed to rearing children nonviolently and hope that if enough people are committed to this, we will break the cycle of violence in society.*

As part of the parenting revolution, we can find creative ways to help children deal with the violence and feelings of fear they may encounter. Many suggestions on how to do this are found throughout this book.

EMPOWERMENT VERSUS ENTRAPMENT

If empowerment is our goal, then what is its opposite? It is the feeling of

- ☞ Being trapped
- ☞ Feeling helpless
- ☞ Feeling out of control

☞ Feeling that life runs us rather than us having a say in how our life unfolds

☞ Feeling that life is happening and we have no ability to change it

The world is full of people, many of whom are children, who feel as if they have no options. Their attitude becomes "I don't care" or "What's the use?" They have lost their dream, a guiding vision for their life, a connection to their gift.

To be aware and believe we have options is the first step in the journey from feeling entrapped to feeling empowered. It is also a mandatory stage to achieve our inner dreams.

EMPOWERED ACTIONS

Empowerment is proactive and involves physically working to manifest our goals and dreams. Our part in assisting children to take empowered actions is to

☞ Encourage them to believe in themselves

☞ Affirm an "I can do it" attitude

☞ Develop the necessary mental focus on the dream

☞ Develop physical skills for follow-through

☞ Define a formula for the success of their dream

Empowerment is future-oriented, built on a belief in our own ability to master whatever is needed at the right moment. Joy Watson speaks as to how her daughter came up with her own formula for success:

When my daughter was three and a half years old, she gave me a secret for empowerment. It was morning shoe time and she was just

at the age where she could put on her shoes but not tie them. I was telling her one morning that she was now big enough to put the shoes on her feet by herself. My part had changed. My part, my responsibility, was just to tie them for her. Someday soon, she'd learn how to tie her laces herself, and then it would be her responsibility to put on her shoes all by herself and tie them, too, just like an adult.

The wisdom of her heartfelt character shined through when she said, "Mommy, I know what an adult is. It's having more and more responsibility and doing more and more things for myself."

My heart opened and I took note of her wisdom. It became another goal of my parenting: to encourage her to follow her own formula for increasing her self-responsibility. That is empowerment in a nutshell!

Empowerment can be expressed by the formula

Belief + Will + Skills = Empowered Actions

This is a winning formula for success. Let us look at the whole formula and particularly at some of the behaviors and skills needed to activate it.

7

Empowered Actions

Belief + Will + Skills = Empowered Actions
Joy Watson

BELIEF IN SELF

When we believe in ourselves, we have confidence in our ability to learn and to master new things. We display the attitude "I can do it!" There are a number of things we can do to encourage this essential quality in our children:

- Speak to them about their strengths.
- Teach them that they're capable of overcoming their fears.
- Assist their learning new skills.
- Model this in our attitude toward them.
- Set up realistic expectations for their successes.
- Shield them from too many failures.
- Witness and value their efforts.
- Support their gifts and their dreams!

So how do we give support?

Annie Haleakala, a wonderful Hawaiian teacher with thirteen children herself, intuitively knew just the right amount of encouragement for each of her children. She taught them to stretch a little higher without failure or feeling overwhelmed. Annie would sit on her stool and each child would have his or her own time with Annie. During each session, she would ask them, "What is the first step to take?" Sometimes, she said, "What is the next step to take?" She would wait for the child to think it through and come up with an answer. Then she would think through their answer by discussion and listening. Almost always Annie ended these special times by saying, "You can do it; I know you can."

A professor of education who had an evening teaching schedule invited one of her four children to dine with her each evening. She spent several hours of intimate conversation and could support each child through listening, conversing, and being present. We can't overlook the importance of what we mean to our children. How can you manage your time to spend quality with your children?

A single father of two girls planned one weekend each quarter for "exploring time." His time with his daughters was spent hiking, camping, exploring nature, and seeing new sites. He took his children away from their everyday environment in order to know their hearts.

And an Italian mother—who cared both for her children and for her elderly parents as well—spent most of her time in the kitchen. Every evening, a different child would cook with her in a relaxed and conversational way. This mother asked hard questions and gave advice. Her children respected her, and they learned to be wonderful cooks!

Truly, children need at least one "other" to support them, to believe in them. Whether this is a parent, caretaker, teacher, friend, or teddy bear, we transfer our power in our beliefs and support. Research by psychologist Raymond Starr Jr. of the University of Maryland confirms that abused or neglected children can escape the cycle of becoming abusive adults: *Nearly 60 percent of the abused or neglected children in the study who now lead productive lives had one nurturing adult as their mentor supporting them emotionally and psychologically.*[1]

We want to encourage children to do what they can without asking so much that they give up or fail. Fostering that "I can do it!" attitude is essential to set up attainable "I did it!" experiences. Here are some helpful activities:

- Ask children to run errands that will end with a happy feeling of "I did it!"
- Ask children to do helpful chores within their abilities so that we can hear the affirmation "Dad, I did it!"
- Ask children questions that will result in our saying, "That's right! Congratulations! You knew the answer!"
- Show them how to do something new, and when they accomplish it, give them a hearty congratulations and a thumbs-up salute.
- Ask children to do things independently, and reflect back, "You did it!"

Remember to keep expectations realistic, breaking tasks into manageable parts so that your children are more likely to succeed in what they do. The idea is to be able to praise them as often as possible for actions of accomplishment and good will.

99

▶ *When our children achieve the small steps, their dream will seem very possible.*

THE WILL TO TAKE ACTION

The more demanding life tasks call for the will to act. This means having the energy, discipline, and perseverance to do whatever it takes to bring the dream into form. This can be the most difficult part of empowerment. We might need to push ourselves, to persevere through mistakes that lead to new learning and growth. This means encouraging children to stay at a task longer than they want and to overcome setbacks.

How can our children persevere through the inevitable difficult moments? Nearly every parent asks this question. Again, the answer lies in realistic expectations.

▶ *We can select tasks for our children that are within their abilities but require them to stretch.*

Breaking down a task into bite-size, doable steps demands awareness and forethought on our part. It may mean giving children a break from the task every twenty minutes so they can refocus their energy and renew concentration. Perhaps it means putting off task completion until another day or pushing to finish it. The goal is to be able to end a session with an honest "Congratulations, you did it!"

▶ *When the goal is empowerment, it is our responsibility to make sure that some form of success results from children's authentic efforts.*

Sometimes we need to push children farther than they are inclined to go. This can usually be done with encouragement rather than with put-downs or threats. Developing the will to take necessary action requires sensitivity, an awareness of when to urge and when to back off.

Children's energy levels are different from ours. They have different neurological processes, which demand frequent breaks for physical movement and energy release. Often it is enough simply to give them a measurable end in sight by saying something like

- ☞ "I know you want to stop now, but I want you to pick up two more toys before taking a break."
- ☞ "Before we take that break you want, let's work just another five minutes. Then we'll have a snack to reward ourselves for our hard work."

In this way, we concentrate on focus while at the same time acknowledging the work the child is accomplishing.

REFLECTIONS

Think about how you speak to your children. Do you ever use loaded statements or put-downs? Was there anything you said today that you would like to change? Make a list now. You want to end with a confirmation for the child rather than a criticism or negation. Change your list now to empowered statements that you can use with children.

Remember and affirm: The goal is lifetime empowerment.

Carol was five when she and her family visited a working ranch. The rancher's daughter was also five and a very capable young equestrian. Carol wanted to be the same. The rancher kindly lifted her onto the horse and guided her around until he encouraged her to trot on her own. As soon as the horse cantered, Carol slid straight off to the ground. When her mother heard her cries, she started over to comfort Carol, but the rancher motioned her to pause. He picked up wailing Carol and put her astride the horse again, saying, "If she doesn't get back on the horse now, she'll be afraid of horses for the rest of her life."

Indeed, she rode again. The rancher slowly walked the horse with Carol in the saddle. When Carol's gripping hands finally relaxed her hold on the rein, the rancher also let go. Carol finally rode the horse on her own.

REFLECTIONS

Remember a time when something was hard for you. How did you handle it? Make a list of the skills you learned about empowerment.

In addition, share the incident with children.

THE SKILLS TO TAKE ACTION

We actively encourage our children to gain empowered, clear-cut thinking skills that are applicable to all successful situations. These include

- Making their decisions
- Acting on their own behalf
- Generating multiple options

☞ Gaining experience in solving "how to" and "what's
next" questions

Our children won't know all the answers or possess all of the
skills at that moment. Rather, they have the confidence that
they can learn specific skills as required and can trust themselves
in the learning process. We want them to feel that they are flexible and intelligent enough to figure out the solutions to life's
problems as they come along.

By asking leading questions, we encourage the creative/
critical thinking that reveals options and generates new ideas.
These questions are open-ended, encouraging children to
respond in more than "yes" or "no" answers. Examples of open-
ended questions (moving from simple to more complex) are

☞ Can you tell me more?
☞ What do you think?
☞ What do you really want?
☞ What is most important to you?
☞ Can you share your ideas with me?
☞ What do you think is possible?
☞ What, if any, may be the consequences of this? Is there
a down side?
☞ What is the worst that can happen?
☞ What would you need to do to make that possible?
☞ What resources and skills do you think you need?
☞ Are you prepared to make mistakes and then still go on?
☞ How will you handle mistakes?
☞ After a mistake, what did you learn from that mistake?
☞ After a success, what did you learn from that success?

☞ What are the long-range effects of a success or a mistake?

☞ Can you imagine any hidden effects that might become known later?

☞ Which bits of information are most important?

☞ Can you imagine something that will affect the outcome?

▶ *Are you willing to coach success skills for life with dedication?*

In Hawaii, fourth-grader Beth wanted to learn how to do Chinese jump rope as well as her friends who had been playing it for years. She had the belief that she could learn and the will to act. What she needed was the specific skill. She spent hours breaking down the game into parts, which she could practice and grow stronger. Before long, Beth felt confident enough to play with the other children, and it became an important part of her life for many months to come. Later, the skills she learned in Chinese jump rope helped her to break the standing broad jump record at her junior high school in California. Beth was doubly empowered.

SELF-AWARENESS AND SELF-ASSESSMENT

Every person has unique learning processes as well as specific difficulties and strengths. Insight into children's learning styles can be taught at a young age to encourage self-awareness.

▶ *Every person has unique learning styles as well as specific difficulties and strengths.*

In a class for teachers on the learning process, the facilitator started the ball rolling, quite literally. She taught juggling as an

enjoyable and fun vehicle for people to observe their own learning process. Juggling is an excellent metaphor for the learning
styles. It requires throwing, catching, and timing, all of which
are separate skills.

Straight three-ball juggling is not very difficult. You can
start with one ball and then add another and another. Very
quickly, children and adults alike see their temperament of
learning: Do they become frustrated easily? Do they enjoy the
learning process? Do they persevere or do they quickly want to
drop out?

Catching is a different skill from throwing the ball, and timing is the last component of the learning task. Juggling allows us
to experience different phases of temperament and learning and
to see how we feel about each one.

As our children learn any new skill, take the time to observe
the way they go about it. It can offer us clues as to how they
approach life, and more importantly, how they approach the
achievement of their dream. Notice their

- Attitudes
- Perseverance levels
- Tolerance for errors
- Enjoyment of successes
- Ability to master one step of the skill and then concen-
  trate on the next step

Ask children to articulate what they are experiencing. It will
show you how they perceive their level of empowerment. Help
them slow down enough to be conscious of their own learning
process and performance.

Children use trial and error much of the time. However, as they mature, they'll learn how to evaluate risks, so that the trial-and-error process becomes more guided and less random. You want to get to the point where the child says things like

- "I thought I'd try this button to see what would happen."
- "I made a mistake, so I did it over again and it came out right."
- "I can see now how I thought it would work because I couldn't see that problem before I started."

SELF-DIRECTED LEARNING

With physical tasks, it is best to let children learn their own way from the very start. This takes the "right way" that has been "shown" to them out of the process. In doing this, you can accelerate the learning process. Coach/trainer Tim Gallwey expects his tennis students to learn the best way to swing the racket on their own. He asks useful questions about what the student was doing when the ball went into the net. Then, when the ball goes over the net, he affirms the success and asks how the student felt. This type of coaching allows the person to assess their own performance and devise their own corrections. It helps the student "feel" their way through an exercise.

The right brain already knows the right way to swing the racket. This knowledge is based on what it feels like to swing the racket to get the result. If Gallwey showed them the "right way," their left-side, analytical brain would be cutting in with external corrections. This can paralyze anyone involved in the learning process. Coach Gallwey has a very high success rate with his students by not cluttering them with style points.

This is the most powerful way to learn anything. "I did it!" is what growing into an achiever is about. This is how children feel empowered to take risks in life and succeed.

The "What Do We Value?" Game

This game is clarifying and empowering, even with small children.

Put up a big piece of poster-board-size paper for each person. Have people start drawing and writing things that are important to them. For little ones, these might include a teddy bear, friend, Mommy, Daddy, or pet. For older children, the list may include the kinds of activities they like: music, recreation, sports, and friends. Or what they value in attitudes and beliefs: Smart people go to college. It's bad to kill animals. Good teachers are friendly.

The idea is for children to become aware of what they really value and believe to be true for their dream to unfold. Many children's beliefs are picked up from television and magazines, so that may be a good place to begin the discussions.

Leave the posters on the back of a door or on the refrigerator to be added to as time passes. Use the values as attitude checks and fuel for personal goal-setting and affirmations.

SUMMARY: THE POWER OF THE WHOLE

▶ *With the development of a mature heart, generosity and true empowerment begin.*

Families are the models for empowerment and holism—honoring of the whole child. A generosity of spirit develops naturally as children grow out of their fears and self-restrictions into a belief in their own power to make wise choices.

When we, both children and adults, become aware of our relationship with all of life and with an inner source of love, intelligence, and guidance, we feel empowered. Becoming aware of an inner source that is greater than ourselves is the ultimate feeling of empowerment. It is a power generated from wholeness and unity with all of creation.

▶ *When we become aware of our relationship with all of life and with an inner source of love, intelligence, and guidance, we feel empowered.*

We develop that awareness of the whole by seeing the larger picture, the dream, and our life purposes. We see relationships as opportunities to learn about caring, love, and respect. As parents, we model this kind of caring in the way we handle the small day-to-day experiences. When we allow our children to make a choice, we can express support rather than doubt. This isn't easy, nor can we expect perfection, either in our children or ourselves. Remember that empowerment is an ideal we hope to attain.

JOURNEY TO THE FUTURE

Here is a series of open-ended questions that we can use at any time to empower possibility! The questions are realistic and yet encourage creative, multiple-option thinking. This sequence can be used with any project or goal simply by adapting the words to fit the situation and the age group.

- Where do you want to go? What is your vision?
- Where are you now? What is your present situation?
- What are the possible ways to go?

- What are the risk factors?
- What is your action plan and strategy for success?
- What are the steps and sequences for action? What tools are needed?
- What can you do every day to turn your vision into a reality?

8

Wholeness: The Mindbody Relationship

Our minds can work for us or against us at any given moment. We can
learn to accept and live with the natural psychological laws that govern
us, understanding how to flow with life rather than struggle against it.
We can return to our natural state of contentment.

Richard Carlson

We must teach our children to dream with their eyes open.

Harry Edwards

We have discussed components of the mindbody system and
their successful development as well as the elements of dream
achievement. One of our tasks as parents is to enable our children to transform their dream, their gift, into a life goal.
Enabling the dream's promise helps it blossom at an appropriate time in children's lives. The last lens through which
we view our children is one of wholeness—seeing how the
mindbody system operates as one unit and applying that
knowledge to help our children manage the mindbody system
throughout life.

THE MINDBODY SYSTEM

The mind and the body are interdependent parts of a complex
living system of cells that communicate with each other. Pio-
neers in biofeedback and cardiology have demonstrated
astounding relationships between our thoughts and the body's

responses, particularly in the cardiovascular and immune systems. We can safely influence physiological functions such as blood flow, heart rate, body temperature, and hormonal secretions by using mental imagery, relaxation, and conscious breathing. These techniques are also effective for stress management, cancer treatments, and pain management.

All of our parts—physical, mental, emotional, and spiritual—are interconnected, each affecting the others. What the mind thinks is activated in each cell. What we feel in one part of the body is immediately communicated to all other cells via neuropeptides. There is no separation between the mind and body, or between the mind and the feelings and emotions.

▶ *The mind exists not only in the brain but also in each and every cell of the body.*

MEDICINE HAS DISCOVERED THE MINDBODY INTERPLAY

It has been verified that the immune system can learn. The immune and central nervous systems communicate biologically with each other. This means that

- ☞ Nothing in our thoughts and emotions is fixed or complete.
- ☞ The mindbody continues to learn throughout life.
- ☞ If what we have learned in the past doesn't serve us, we can relearn positive patterns that do.

Daniel Goleman writes, "The mind, the emotions, and the body [are] not separate, but intimately entwined."[1]

In the past fifteen years, psychoneuroimmunologists have demonstrated that the immune system is affected by, and directly related to, the central nervous system as well as to the brain and endocrine system.

▶ *Emotions are learned responses within the interplay of our chemicals and hormones. They form a biochemical imprint on our mindbody system.*

These patterns are body memories that cause repetitions of our reactions and thoughts. Repetitious thoughts and emotional memories can be reeducated, which has a significant impact on enabling emotions to serve as a bridge to our dreams.

THE PSYCHOSOMATIC NETWORK

In the 1980s, it was proven that short chains of amino acids called neuropeptides extend throughout the body.[2] Neuropeptides carry information to and between cells and can alter cell function.

The organs and the various body systems—immune, endocrine, digestive, respiratory, cardiovascular, and so on—hold and convey feelings and memories and can store information. Information and feelings are transferred from cell to cell, creating a psychosomatic (thought/body) network. The body is now known to be a dynamic processor of energy in the form of thought and emotions.[3]

MANAGING EMOTIONS IS A KEY TO BALANCE

We express ourselves emotionally in a variety of ways such as speaking, drawing, painting, journaling, exercising, visualizing, eating, and in acupuncture, walking, and breathing. *Appropriately expressing emotions moves energy that is stuck in the mindbody system.*

▶ *The movement or expression of emotional energy balances and relaxes the mindbody system.*

Managing emotions is just one way for us to stay calm and unstressed. All emotions serve a positive purpose to help people express themselves and, therefore, are potentially life-affirming.[4]

It is not the emotions themselves but the way that we manage them which can help us affirm life and achieve our dream. We also can use the power of imagery, language, breathing, and thought to influence the body. Athletes create mental pictures of their bodies successfully performing specific activities. That mental focus heightens their ability to perform and increases their intrinsic motivation to achieve.

Understanding the mindbody connection helps us take charge of our lives, our health, and our sense of well-being. We can cause changes in our negative thought patterns by using such skills as affirmations, guided imagery, and relaxation, which are discussed in depth in the successive chapters. We also can assist our children to be more aware of their thoughts to learn how to alter their causes of stress, anxiety, depression, and psychosomatic symptoms. Our children *can* achieve their dreams and, in focusing on the positive, create more joy and enhance their sense of well-being.

BELIEF AND EXPECTATION

Our beliefs mirror what we think about ourselves and about the world, but they can also become our truths whether or not they have any basis in current reality, much like a child's egocentric belief that he is the cause of his parents' divorce.

▶ *Beliefs determine how we feel about ourselves and how we react to the world around us.*

If we are told repeatedly as children and teenagers that we are stupid, then we believe it to be so, whether or not it is true. The belief remains in our subconscious data banks until we change its content or choose not to listen. We may settle for mediocrity and forget that the extraordinary dream our heart holds needs fire and passion and joy for its expression.

As adults, we mentally replay the tapes of our parents' messages repeatedly, unless we recognize and change our beliefs to erase the old data from our memory and input new information. Often we don't even remember where our erroneous beliefs came from, but that really doesn't matter.

▶ *What matters is that we become aware of our limiting beliefs and help our children to do the same—and then make an affirming choice to change what doesn't work.*

Suppose six-year-old Eric breaks his younger brother's toy fire truck. Our response might be, "Eric, why can't you behave? You're always breaking things!" Here we tell Eric that we expect him to keep breaking things. The message which Eric records is that he always misbehaves and breaks things. His belief receives confirmation as his destructive behavior continues.

A more loving response might be, "Eric, it is just not like you to break Colin's fire truck!" Notice the difference? Eric's belief that he doesn't usually act this way is being reinforced, and we convey the information that this is unusual behavior for him, so what's up? His future behavior is more likely to conform to this expectation, and he will be less likely to act out his destructive impulses.

Seven-year-old Jessica came home from her first day of second grade with a stomachache. It lasted well into the next

115

day, causing her to miss school. Jessica was convinced that she didn't feel well despite the doctor's opinion that she seemed fine. Jessica's father awakened early the next morning and invited Jessica to get dressed and go to breakfast with him at a local diner. The father expected Jessica would like to go, and she did. The opportunity to spend time with her father delighted her.

At breakfast, Jessica's father commented several times about how bright and healthy she looked. Jessica responded to her father's caring by visibly sitting up straighter and smiling. That morning her father took her to school.

The father did not nag, cajole, or get stressed out about sending her to school sick. He was aware that she wasn't really sick. He chose an affirming method of getting her to school the next day. And it worked!

We may not always know what thoughts muse in our children's heads and cause their bodies to not feel well. However, we can observe the small clues and choose an appropriate method to help our children feel safe and loved again. It isn't always necessary to dig through the "How do you feel?" and "Why do you feel that way?" discussions. Sometimes, verbal recognition and kindness or positive expectations might be all they need.

MESSAGES FROM THE BODY

Children's beliefs about themselves affect their self-esteem and confidence level as well as their behavior and abilities. We can instill in our children self-beliefs that nurture and uplift them, affirm their self-esteem, and give them the confidence they need to grow into healthy adults. To do this, we need to understand how our own beliefs affect our lives. Since our bodies and minds are connected, we can look to our body for clues to beliefs we may hold subconsciously.

THE MINDBODY CONNECTION

Our subconscious beliefs register in our bodies. Sometimes the physical clues are quite literal:

- ☞ If we have back problems, we might wonder what areas of our lives we are backing out of or what burdens we believe we are carrying on our backs. Maybe our back says that we don't feel supported.
- ☞ If our legs are giving us problems, perhaps we aren't standing up for ourselves in some areas of our lives. Maybe we feel stuck or don't want to move ahead with something.
- ☞ If we are having stomach problems, it could be something in our lives we're having trouble digesting.
- ☞ If our throat is sore, there may be something we are not expressing.

It is important to coach our children to take charge of and direct their thoughts and to rely on and believe in their inherent abilities. The more positively children think about themselves, the more aware they will be of the possibilities of their unfolding dream and the more courageous and enthusiastic they can be about their unfolding futures.

▶ *A positive emotional/mental state sends healthy messages to the body.*

Have you noticed how easily others join us if we are angry, depressed, or spewing negative words and thoughts? When we stay aware, we can *choose* to become positive or negative. Simply

117

by thinking positive thoughts and speaking positive words, we attract positive energy. There is awesome power in thought and its ability to affect the body.

REFLECTIONS

Within your household and family, what kind of mental input feeds your child's beliefs? What kinds of statements do you use with your child? What language do you observe among his peers? What television shows are her favorites? What chat rooms does/would she visit on the Internet? If you are not satisfied or happy with your list, write down some affirmative actions to make changes. Decide when will you start making those changes.

STRESS AND HEALING

Four-year-old Lindy is enrolled in a full-day nursery school. Because her parents leave for work before the school day begins, they take Lindy to a neighbor who watches her until her car pool takes her to school at 9 A.M. After school, Lindy goes back to the neighbor's house until her parents pick her up at 6 P.M. Lindy is away from home for ten hours, during which time she has had to adjust to a number of different environments and people. All of these changes are a lot for a four-year-old to deal with. It is not surprising, then, that Lindy is fussy at school. She is suffering from stress.

Rich, an eighth grader, dreads the start of the school year. A bright, sociable student, Rich has been unusually quiet and withdrawn during most of the summer. When pressed by his parents for an explanation, Rich blurts, "I don't want to get beat up by the druggies at school." His anxiety is caused by a legitimate fear of possible danger at school. Like Lindy, Rich is under stress.

► *Stress is an event in a child's life that causes imbalance to the body or emotions, alters development, or threatens a child's security or safety.*

In recent decades, the number and severity of childhood stressors has increased. Cultural changes have altered the work and social structures of the family system in such a way that children have fewer sources of adult support, affirmation, and love available than in the past.

Problems begin when ordinary stress becomes too much stress. When under duress, the heart rate and breathing speed up and muscles tighten. Multiple sources of stress worsen the level and duration of the stress. Our bodies need relief from stress to reestablish balance.

Stressful encounters and their resolution are natural human processes, and feelings of anxiety are normal emotions, which, when handled well, can be character-building. Stress becomes damaging only if it is traumatic, overwhelming, or is not addressed.

► *Part of growing up is coping effectively with stress.*

SYMPTOMS OF STRESS

Children's stress symptoms differ among age ranges. Eugene Arnold writes

> *Typically, preschoolers lack self-control, have no sense of time, act independently, are curious, may wet the bed, have changes in eating*

habits, have difficulty with sleep or speech, and cannot tell adults how they are feeling.

Preschoolers under stress each react differently. Some behaviors may include irritability, anxiety, uncontrollable crying, trembling with fright, eating or sleep problems.

Toddlers may regress to infant behaviors, feel angry and not understand their feelings, fear being alone or without their parent, withdraw, bite, or be sensitive to sudden or loud noises. Feelings of sadness or anger may build inside of them. They may become angry or aggressive, have nightmares, or be accident-prone.

Typical elementary-age children can whine when things don't go their way, be aggressive, question adults, try out new behaviors, complain about school, have fears and nightmares, and lose concentration.

Reactions to stress may include withdrawal, feelings of being unloved, being distrustful, not attending to school or friendships, and having difficulty naming their feelings. Under stress, they may worry about the future, complain of head or stomachaches, have trouble sleeping, have a loss of appetite, or need to urinate frequently.[5]

Children can be subjected to stress at home when their parents are under the pressure of career and personal fulfillment competing with family for time and space. Changing expectations within the family can lead to tension as women take their place in the work world and as mothers and fathers struggle with role definitions. Pressures are often heightened in the single-parent home when one parent takes responsibility for both parenting roles.

THE IMPACT OF THE MEDIA

The media, especially television, places its own brand of stress on children by presenting them with too much information, which is often too complex for them to understand. While children in the United States ranks poorly on international surveys designed to measure academic achievement, they are leading their global counterparts in television viewing, ranking first in the percentage of thirteen-year-olds who watch five or more hours of television a day. Unlike reading, watching television allows children little or no time for reflection and processing.

Billy's father was called to active duty in the Persian Gulf. For weeks the nine-year-old could think of nothing but the war. He was surrounded by it from the time he awoke until the time he went to bed. First thing in the morning, his mother turned on the radio for the current news. Arriving at school one-half hour early on the bus, Billy waited in the gymnasium where the television blared more war news. At home every evening, there was more of the same.

With this intense media bombardment, no one thought to give Billy an opportunity to get in touch with his emotions or talk about what was on his mind. After a couple of weeks, because he could not consciously get a handle on what was happening, Billy's unconscious took over. He began to have nightmares. Teachers noticed him "acting out" at school. A child psychologist determined that Billy's stress stemmed from informational and emotional overload. Having his father away from home during the war was stressful enough, but the continued media coverage only confounded his stress and enlivened his fear. Billy said he "saw pictures of war in his head, day and night." The pictures on the television relived themselves in his mind until they became nightmares.

How Stress Impacts the Body

When we are under stress, our bodies react by calling on energy reserves to adapt to the situation at hand. Adrenaline pumps into the blood, heart and breathing rates quicken, digestion stops, and blood pressure rises. We may not even notice these things taking place during stressful events, but we are likely to feel them afterward as we complain of feeling drained and run-down. When your children exhibit these symptoms, coach them in abdominal breathing exercises (see chapter 10).

With the proper rest and exercise, a fit body will automatically replenish its energy supply once the stress response runs its course. A body that takes repeated abuse without the necessary rest and exercise, however, will eventually show signs of distress in the form of mild to severe health problems. Sadly, a growing number of children today are showing the symptoms of these so-called stress diseases.

▶ *The mindbody connection shows us that when the body falls out of balance, the mind follows.*

Helen was sexually abused when she was a child. Her uncle repeatedly said to her, "You are a bad girl." She believed this voice in her head and acted it out as a teenager. One night when she was desperate, she started praying. Immediately another picture came into her head. She was dressed in a ballerina's long white dress and was dancing around the basement of her home. Overnight she became a different youth. She actually started dancing in her basement all by herself to express the knotted pain in her belly. A family friend offered to teach her popular folk and modern dances. Soon she became a member of her community's folk-arts-festival dancers. The new image was powerful and gave her hope.

HELPING CHILDREN MANAGE STRESS

Physical Fitness

Maintaining physical fitness helps ready the body to deal with stressful situations when they arise. One way to ensure children's physical fitness is to teach by example. Children who see their parents exercise are inclined to exercise, too. Encourage children's participation in sports of their choice.

Yoga, dance, simple stretches, exercises, and body movement are all popular methods that can be explored. (See stretching exercises at the end of chapter 10.) Movement is natural, especially for young children. It helps to keep children fit, but it also teaches them to explore their surroundings and helps them relate to direction and space. Child-development experts agree that play is crucial to a child's physical and mental well-being, and play therapy is used to help children reframe emotionally traumatic events.

Mental Fitness

Exercise for the body is only part of the answer to stress. In today's pressure-packed culture, mind fitness is as important as body fitness. While physiological changes affect one's mental/emotional state, thoughts and feelings affect the body's ability to rejuvenate and heal. Today's children need to develop

123

appropriate mechanisms for managing stress—ones that take into account the intimate relationship between mind and body. ▶ *Relaxation may be the single most important step in managing daily stress.*

When children are relaxed, several things take place in the body: the heartbeat slows down; the body's electrical system, as evidenced by brain-wave activity, slows down; and the mind quiets. When children relax, they learn that their behavior is influenced internally and that they have some control over their feelings.

The author, in collaboration with Joy Watson, parent and educator, has developed a program called Mind Fitness™. This program includes relaxation exercises that parents can use with children of all ages. Once children are relaxed and their minds quieted, parents help them create positive mental images through visualization, affirmation, movement, and expression, all of which train a fit mind and are discussed in subsequent chapters.

Some of the stress children encounter today stems from an inability to let go of negative images such as those on the news depicting environmental ruin or world hunger. At other times, children may not be aware of the images they hold but can pinpoint the emotions associated with failure, fear, or loneliness.

Self-directed imagery or guided stories, during which we visualize positive images and hold them in our minds, are powerful tools for managing stress and emotional states. These can be coupled effectively with affirmations, which are positive statements of one's goals.

Kimberly, age ten, was upset because her father called to say he'd be late picking her up again. It seemed that every Saturday when he was supposed to take her for the day, he called with some excuse to be late. One day she had to wait an extra hour because he said there was something urgent he had to take care of at his office.

Kimberly's mother knew that her former husband meant well, but she also understood that he expected too much of Kimberly not to take his repeated lateness to heart. She decided to help Kimberly deal with her frustration by using a guided imagery for "clearing feelings." This imagery helped Kimberly pinpoint the areas in her body where she was feeling tense and replaced the discomfort and negativity with bright light. Later, they discussed Kimberly's feelings and created ways she could express them to her father. Kimberly acknowledged that those "bad" feelings were likely to surface again, but she saw that she had the power to replace them with positive ones whenever she wanted.

Kimberly's mother taught her the power of being aware and making choices for her well-being. Other techniques that we can use with children include storytelling, creative visualization, and creative drama. Music and breathwork also relieve stress almost instantly. All of these techniques are discussed in later chapters.

If these techniques sound simple, it's because they are. Children are naturally resilient and resourceful. Given the proper encouragement, love, and guidance, they can cope with much of the stress they encounter on a daily basis.

To achieve our dreams, the mindbody system must be in good health. We want to be able to express expansive emotions and to be mentally focused. We ask no less of our children every day of their lives, yet we fail to provide them with easy and effective tools like how to relax, how to think through a problem, how to be proactive, and how to show compassion. These are aspects of esteem, empowerment, and wholeness—building blocks for dream achievement.

The following chapters provide tools for rearing successful and happy children—mental fitness, breath, and music. We suggest you use one chapter at a time as a teaching tool for yourself and then coach your children in these lifelong management skills.

Part Three

Tools That Restore Wholeness

and Foster the Gift:

Mental Fitness,

Breath,

and Music

9

Mental Fitness

Nothing is as real as a dream. The world can change around you,
but your dream will not. Responsibilities need not erase it.
Duties need not obscure it. Because the dream is
within you, no one can take it away.

Tom Clancy

NOTICING OUR THOUGHTS

How many of us look in the mirror in the morning and say, "I am beautiful and healthy, and I really feel good about myself"? More often it's "I am so fat and old and ugly" or "Look at all of those wrinkles!" or "Another day, ho hum."

When we say contrary things to ourselves, our bodies respond immediately with sagging posture. We feel depressed and our outlook for the day becomes negative. This isn't a particularly joyful way to start our day.

REFLECTIONS

Test this out for yourself. Starting tomorrow, begin *each* day by saying something positive about yourself while looking in the mirror. Celebrate yourself! Be sure to smile. Then, over the

coming weeks, notice any differences in how you
feel and how you perceive yourself.

When we smile, our bodies cannot be depressed. Just a simple smile sends a positive picture to our mindbody system. What happens when we smile and say something positive about ourselves? The body straightens, the smile releases tension, and we feel better. Even if another voice in the head says, "I don't believe that," it doesn't matter. The body and emotions have responded to the positive, affirming image of ourselves that we have chosen.

The more often we do affirm life, think openly, and feed the system positive fuel, the less we'll hear from our doubting voice. Soon the new thoughts and feelings shape different perceptions within us. Our outlook changes, and our world is different. This is the power of the thought and feeling in the body! It was once said that pessimists have a firm grip on reality, but optimists live longer, are healthier, and are better liked.

USING AFFIRMATIONS

Affirmations are positive, empowering statements that affirm what we want our perception of reality to be. They are effective in changing our thoughts and beliefs. There are many ways we can use affirmations with our children.

When we are talking with them about something they have done well, we can simply say, "Let's close our eyes for a second and see that moment of success in our mind. Affirm: *I did it well*."

At nighttime, we might lead our children on a verbal dream trail of accomplishing something successful. Tell them a story that is full of good feelings. It might be something like "Let's close our eyes and see if you can imagine everything I say. You are in a forest that is full of sweet smells, the light is shining through the trees in a special and wonderful way, and there are many birds singing. Hear them chirping? Now run and do a flip in perfect form. Feel yourself take five fast steps, and then raise your arms over your head and spring off the ground and turn! Feel your hands touching the firm ground. Now roll over so you're back on your feet. See how well you did that! You are successful. Affirm: *I am successful at doing things that I want to do.*"

HOW TO WORD AFFIRMATIONS

Just about anything can be affirmed, but there are guidelines that strengthen an affirmation.

1. *Avoid stating intentions or goals negatively.* Children can say, "I am a graceful ballet dancer" rather than "I am not a bad dancer." This keeps the focus on the desired results and avoids giving attention to "bad dancing."

2. *Say or write affirmations in the first person.* For instance, children can say, "I successfully completed my test" instead of "My teacher will give me a good grade on my test." By coaching your children to focus positively on themselves, you teach them that they *earn* their successes. You empower them to invest in themselves.

3. *State affirmations in the present tense,* even if the event has not yet happened, to strengthen the assertion. Like runners who see themselves crossing the finish line first before a race, have your child imagine success. Putting an

affirmation in the present tense creates mental tension when the event or state of being hasn't yet occurred. To relieve this tension, we must act on our affirmation. Saying that we have already run, and won, a race, when in fact the race hasn't yet occurred, motivates us to run harder and faster than we might have otherwise. The brain is saying to the body, "Do it this way." It provides a mental rehearsal for our performance.

4. *State affirmations clearly and to the point.* The shorter and simpler the affirmation, the more effective it is. If it is too wordy, it will quickly lose its impact. It is more powerful to say, "I am an imaginative writer" rather than "My friends think I am a really neat writer because I come up with all kinds of make-believe creatures with cool names." Even if children are able to remember the second affirmation, they aren't likely to feel motivated by it.

5. *Repeat affirmations often* and they work! This can be aloud or internally.

6. *Put heartfelt emotions behind affirmations* to give them punch to motivate us.

7. *Personalize the affirmations.* What works for one person may not work for another. If an affirmation doesn't feel right, play with the words until it does.

We don't even need a compelling reason to use affirmations. They can be used anytime to enhance one's sense of giftedness and esteem. However, they can be especially effective for children during times of emotional or mental stress, like before a big game or an important test. By training our children to use these techniques and then reminding them to use them, we give them a powerful tool that is always available.

The following story illustrates just how powerful affirmations can be, even in times of crisis.

> *One day when my daughter Kris was eleven, she and I decided to go hiking. We reached the summit of the mountain within three hours. After resting and eating lunch, we were ready to descend and wanted to find the quickest way down. We came upon a steep ledge, which I descended first. When Kris saw me below her, she froze in fear. No matter how much I coaxed her to follow, I couldn't get her to say anything more than "I can't."*
>
> *I began to sing an affirmation, "I go over the rock, and I sing and climb down." At first, Kris began to sing along with me, in effect shifting her focus away from fear and breaking the paralysis caused by too much thinking. As she sang, Kris slowly made her way over the ledge with much trepidation. Singing the affirmation led Kris to a successful descent, even if she didn't believe it at the time. Telling her body to move by affirming it made it happen.*

FEARS AND DOUBTS

Here's a scenario. We teach our child to choose a simple, positive affirmation that feels right for him, such as, " I am a good softball player," and we encourage him to repeat it. It seems to be working. Then on the day before the big tryouts, he comes home from school full of doubt. "I can't catch worth beans, Dad. I'll never make the team."

We all have inner voices full of doubts and fears, fueled by memories of past failures. These voices undermine our best intentions to think positively.

▶ *It's important to acknowledge and accept negative emotions without having to act them out.*

Ask him what he is feeling and reflect what you hear back to him. Encourage him to accept and experience these feelings without trying to change them. Too many adults suffer the ill effects of having stuffed their emotions as children. No matter how trivial they may seem to us, our children's feelings need to be acknowledged and accepted without indulging them.

During these times of insecurity, affirmations can play a role. Use them to inspire a different outlook or new point of view in your child. If faced with the situation above, acknowledge that your son lacks confidence in his catching ability. Tell him again that you believe he can do it, but you understand he has doubts. Describe for him an occasion when you yourself lacked confidence. Show empathy, and then suggest that his catching will improve with practice. Perhaps a plan of action to improve his skills will improve his self-esteem. The point here is not to convince your son that he is an all-star. Rather, your goal is to help your child to be willing, to try, and to persevere.

Alternatively, find a strength that he can affirm. Maybe he's a great hitter, so remind him of this. Encourage him to remind himself of it every day. He might change his affirmation from "I am a good softball player" to "I am a good hitter" and "Every day my catching improves."

▶ *Affirmations create a positive and hopeful lens through which our children can view their world.*

REFLECTIONS

Create a mental picture of crossing a river, first for yourself and later with your child. Encourage the mental vision of the two of you actively working to "cross the river" together. See, and perhaps draw, a picture of the boat you both share and the oar in each of your hands. When crisis occurs, use this metaphor to determine a solution.

Affirm: Together we are actively embracing the skills and confidence to reach our goals.

Another approach that can be taken when children are feeling they can't do "it"—whatever "it" might be—is to help them remember a time when they thought something was impossible yet they got through it. Together, play back the scenario as it happened just as the "Reflections" section shows you. What did they tell themselves back then? How did they get through it? Can those same affirmations be modified and used now?

LESSONS LEARNED

Life is full of challenges and growing experiences. As aware parents, we teach our children to appreciate the lessons learned along the way and to store them for future use. Once children have mastered situation x by using skills y and z, they can use those same skills whenever a new situation arises.

Like pearls of wisdom, affirmations are small yet valuable. Children can create simple affirmations that they can repeat. Repetition anchors the positive emotion in the mindbody system. Affirm each individual in the family during regular gatherings, such as dinner: "Our family works well together. We are a team who love and respect one another."

GUIDED IMAGERY: A MAGIC KEY

Who knows what lurks in the minds of our children? Adventure heroes with super powers? Mutant aliens who explore far-off spaces? Friendly angels who protect them from the darkness? It is these mythic figures from children's imaginations that help us to help them.

Rather than venture an educated guess when symptoms like withdrawal, poor eating, or acting-out occur, it is much easier to give children the magic key to open their mindbody connection to see what is really going on in their heart and head. One therapist tells this story:

> *Twelve-year-old Jeff was discouraged by his unsuccessful attempts to pass science tests. Science phobia set in. He didn't want to go to class, complete homework, or study the subject. The more his parents wanted to talk about it, the more silent he became. When they reminded him of homework and the science fair, he went to his room in silence. Jeff had built a wall, and no one could penetrate it. Why scale the wall in a frontal attack when we can sneak in through the door of his imagination?*
>
> *As his therapist, I asked Jeff to sit comfortably, unwind, and close his eyes. After speaking to his body about relaxing and feeling safe, I ask him to imagine a super hero who could take care of his problems.*
>
> *His imagination soared and his vision opened as he described an intergalactic ship captain who sped to the assistance of boys in*

despair. The hero had super hearing and vision that could penetrate density. His silver uniform protected him from temperature and barometric changes as well as from external assault.

I guided Jeff to ask the hero to solve the problem of the poor science grades and incomplete homework. The hero took him on an intergalactic flight to another planet where Jeff was the scientist making great discoveries to help humanity. The superhero told Jeff that this could be his future, but he would have to start now to gain all of the knowledge necessary to become his dream. Before I could even suggest that he open his eyes, Jeff popped up from the chair and exclaimed, "I knew it!"

Jeff's imagination gave him the image and impetus to get moti-vated. Through his imagery, Jeff gleaned a hint for his future. Was this his dream? We didn't discuss any more. I thanked him for his cooperation, and he went home with his mother.

Jeff's attitude toward science class changed significantly. No wonder he took his failure so personally! His mother later reported that his grades were average, but his renewed enthusiasm was A+. Jeff had reached inside to find a part of his own strength, personified it, and discovered his own answers. The use of imagination is often more effective than any lecture we can give.

THE POWER OF THE IMAGINATION

The imagination is a key to communication and problem solving. It is important to approach it with the clearest intention of allowing children all the time and space needed inside of them to figure it out. In our busy worlds and intellectual pursuits, we often forget this magic key: *Sharing time and stories of mythic heroes and inner worlds can restore harmony in relationships.*

Think how far the Industrial Revolution has brought our Western traditions from the early-evening family gatherings where stories were shared and children were given time to exercise their imaginations. Our parenting revolution can restore what we value of our traditions. A teacher of learning-disabled children explained how storytelling and imagination helped one student learn:

> *When I taught the learning-disabilities class at a junior high school, one hyperactive student had gifted intelligence but couldn't understand what he read. He had a visual processing problem. He listened to lessons on tape, took notes, and used his photographic memory to compensate for lack of comprehension. Despite his friendly manner and winning personality, he carried a deep depression that he shared only with his mother and me.*
>
> *One day I asked him to close his eyes and make himself very small, tiny enough to drift like a boat through the bloodstream of his body so he could see what was going on inside. In no time at all he was zooming to his spine. What he described to me was incredible. "Yes, I can see my nervous system, and I will report to you, captain. Sir, it is amazing, like a huge electrical circuit has been disconnected along the spine. Electrical energy is flying everywhere, sir. If I get any closer, I will be electrocuted. Sir, what should I do?"*
>
> *Of course, I couldn't ruin his adventure by telling him what to do. Therefore, I turned the question back to him. "Mate, I can only rely on your competence to solve this problem. Do the best that you can! Be careful. I'm counting on you!"*

He continued to describe the specific areas along the spine where energy flare-ups occurred, and he put them out as if they were wildfires. He fixed all the energy disturbances by readjusting the spine with special tools and rebuilding neural pathways for new energy flow and smoother conduction. Finally, he reported in.

"I made it, sir. Problems solved. Request permission to return to base."

"Permission granted."

This young man learned a unique lesson and invaluable tool. He identified his version of his learning problem—energy flare-ups along the spine. Then he made up his own story. When he felt hyperactive and inattentive, he closed his eyes, went to his spine, and fixed the problem with his special tools. When he felt tired from hours of studying, he used the same affirming inner journey to refocus his mind. He discovered a path to ease learning and a tool to compensate for the hyperactivity that his body could not control.

We can use guided imagery and stories to help children see pictures in their head for specific benefits. Our goal is to create positive, healthy outcomes. For example, to help a child feel safe, we might have her visualize being in her favorite spot. Images in our mind can evoke the same physical and emotional sensations that real situations do. For instance, a fearful image can cause our pulse to quicken, or our blood pressure to get higher, or our mouth to get dry. As demonstrated by biofeedback techniques, creating a relaxing image can lower the heart rate, lower the blood pressure, and relax the muscles.[1] Guided imagery can produce positive outcomes and relaxed emotions.

We can also lead children through stories that tap into their creativity. A story can take them to a nurturing place that feels comforting, like their favorite tree house. Here they can learn to relax, build feelings of self-worth, solve problems, and so on.

If the desired outcome is relaxation, we might guide them to a beach with lulling waves or to a field of colorful flowers. To solve problems, the children could visualize a large television screen before them where they are coached to see an announcer coming on to give them an answer. This technique works very well for children who can remember how words look when spelled correctly but can't determine correct spelling through phonics. As we become more familiar with the process, we will be able to use guided stories with our children to enhance various situations.

Perhaps the greatest benefit of guided imagery lies in the potential for developing self-esteem and a belief in one's ability to effect change for the better.

▶ *Children who can visualize themselves in a positive way have taken the first step toward actualizing their dream.*

PRINCIPLES AND TECHNIQUES OF GUIDED IMAGERY

One of the principles behind techniques such as relaxation, guided stories, and imagery is to calm the active brain waves for receptivity and learning. At later points in the book, we will discuss how the most effective learning takes place in a relaxed and alert state. There are four basic categories of brain waves:

1. Beta waves are found in our normal waking state of consciousness and vibrate at frequencies of 14 to 20 cycles per second (Hz).

2. Next are alpha waves, from 8 to 13 Hz, which occur when we daydream or meditate. It is the space we are in between sleeping and being fully conscious and awake. This alpha, or relaxed, level is the state we work within while using guided imagery.

3. The third category of brain waves is theta waves, from 4 to 7 Hz, which occur in states of very deep meditation and sleep.

4. The fourth category is delta waves, from 0.5 to 3 Hz, which occur in deep sleep and have been found in very profound states of healing or meditation.

Guided imagery is a powerful tool and yet quite simple to learn and to share with our children. We can introduce guided imagery into their lives by helping them enter a relaxed frame of mind at the alpha level. This is the most effective state when using guided imagery because the mind is relaxed, receptive, and yet alert. It helps children grasp this idea by giving them a concrete image. For example, you might tell them that relaxing their minds is like shaking all of the contents of their head into a garbage can. After the children relax, guide them through a story or journey. The purpose and direction of the story will vary depending on what we want to accomplish.

The following instructions and examples describe the process of using guided imagery. Once we feel comfortable with the process, we can create our own stories and journeys or co-create stories with our children. This process gives everyone a chance to be creative. Make sharing guided imagery a part of the normal family routine and enjoy the gifts it brings.

STEPS FOR CREATING A GUIDED JOURNEY

Step 1: Relaxation and Induction

The first step in using guided imagery is to have children relax either by sitting comfortably or by lying down. Younger children may even want to sit in our laps. If some children seem restless, we might gently touch them, putting our hand on their shoulder or belly, or rock with them. With little ones we might do the guided imagery just before nap time or bedtime when they are winding down. We can also use it as a bedtime story.

Instruct them to close their eyes and to breathe deeply. Some younger children may not be able to keep their eyes shut. This is OK. To help them accomplish deep rhythmic breathing, suggest that they put their hand on their belly and see if they can move it up and down as they breathe in and out. Also, refer to the next chapter on breathing for more benefits of this approach.

To help them relax their body, tell them to wiggle and then relax each part of their bodies. Start by wiggling their toes, then their feet, then their legs, buttocks, stomach, chest, arms, fingers, shoulders, back, neck, and face. This will help them release any tension in their bodies.

Another relaxation method is for children to imagine each part of their body falling asleep or resting. One mother told me she guides her daughter to imagine her body feeling heavy and sinking into the mattress. We can also do simple and easy relaxation methods such as taking five deep breaths, leaning over from the waist, hanging to relax, and imagining that we're floating on a cloud.

Some children tend to go into a relaxed state quite easily, whereas others seem energetic and don't want to relax. With energetic children, we can find a time of day that works better or put on some fast-moving, fun music and dance to release some of the energy. Then try relaxing into a guided journey.

For particularly active or sensitive children, let them tell you a story that relaxes them rather than imposing a specific approach. For example, seven-year-old Joseph went on overload very easily after a lot of stimulus, excitement, or activity. One day he said to his parents during a soccer game, "I have to be by myself now and settle down." He went to the car, breathed deeply to relax, and quieted himself. After ten minutes, he returned to the soccer game with more focus and enthusiasm. His parents simply accepted their son's approach, and Joseph continued this behavior well into his teen years.

Step 2: Guidelines for Guided Stories

Next, we can guide children through the story or journey, perhaps using one of the sample stories below or by making up our own. Children access their imaginations easily.

When guiding these stories, be sure to

1. Read slowly, pausing after each sentence to allow time for children to see the images.
2. Use a soothing tone of voice.
3. Keep the stories short and simple, especially for preschool children.
4. Use concrete images they can understand, simple language, and short explanations.

5. Involve as many of the senses as possible. For example, you might say, "Feel the soft breeze caress the cheek, smell the pine trees, hear the birds, see the blue sky." Tying in physical sensory images is important for children. Sample stories are provided later in this section.

When first working with guided stories, it is often helpful to tape-record the journey and experience it personally before using it with our children. This gives us better feelings for the rhythm, pace, and tones to use while guiding children through the process.

We can use these journeys to help children

- ☞ Relax and sleep
- ☞ Prepare for an upcoming test or sports event
- ☞ Assist in healing their body
- ☞ Understand their schoolwork
- ☞ Build their sense of worth and confidence
- ☞ Solve problems
- ☞ Tap into their creative abilities
- ☞ Connect with their inner wisdom
- ☞ Explore, be creative, and have fun
- ☞ Know, discover, and activate the dream!

Step 3: Closing

At the end of the journey or story, make sure to have children return to an active brain wave state by inviting them back to the present. For example, if we are guiding children who are resting in bed, have them feel themselves back in their bed. Tell them to bring the good feelings back into their body now. Suggest they wiggle their toes or fingers. Have them count aloud to five with us. The purpose of closing the story is to end the session and bring closure to the exercise. We coach them to return from the alpha state back into the beta state, their normal, wakeful state of mind.

Step 4: Process the Experience

Once the journey has ended, take time to discuss the experience. This may simply mean talking with them about it to reach a deeper understanding. We might ask what they saw or felt while on the journey. They can draw pictures of their experience or dance their narration. Many older children love to journal and use creative drama, whereas preschoolers prefer concrete, tangible, simple exercises. For example, if in the journey they visualized themselves as a special star, then make a star with them out of colored paper and glitter. If the guided journey brought them in touch with an inner hero, we might have them go outside and find a special rock that reminds them of this special inner friend. Allow time and space for children to share their experience in whatever way seems appropriate.

Sometimes children will see images they don't understand. We can help them figure out what they might represent. One mother shared a story of how she did this.

After years of absence, her daughter's father was coming back into her life. Simultaneously the girl developed a fever. Knowing the situation was creating stress for her daughter, the mother coached her through a guided relaxation. While the daughter was relaxing, story images emerged in which she saw herself going to the hospital in an ambulance. In the image, she

145

died in the ambulance. The mother felt this image was a metaphor for something deeper.

It was vital for the mother to help her daughter figure out what this image might mean. Sharing their feelings about the father and talking about the event made them realize that change in one's life is often symbolized by death: the old way is dying to make room for the new. The mother was aware that the upcoming change in her daughter's life was frightening her in some ways. She again guided her back into a quiet space and told her to wait for an image to illustrate what the change in her life will be like. The image the daughter got this time was of her walking very happily and confidently down a new street.

This process helped the daughter see that change, although frightening, can become a path on which she feels happy and confident. Letting go of the old makes room for pleasant new situations to enter. As old situations die, new ones are born.

SAMPLE GUIDED JOURNEYS

Now take a look at some sample guided journeys. The first is an adaptation of a journey that a mother shared with me. She found this helpful when her young daughter was having trouble sleeping at night.

Journey to Sleep

Get very comfortable . . . take a deep breath . . . feel your belly rising and falling with your breath . . . breathe in and out deeply . . . know you are safe and loved . . . let your body get very heavy . . . it is so heavy it feels as if you are sinking into the mattress . . . imagine you are walking down a path . . . it leads to the woods . . .

it is a bright sunny day . . . you feel peaceful and happy . . . you look and see that a dog is walking with you . . . reach out to touch and pet him . . . feel his soft fur . . . and you both keep walking along the path . . . see the blue sky . . . smell the wildflowers . . . hear birds chirping . . . the path leads you to some stairs . . . climb up . . . and up . . . at the top see a big white cloud . . . and jump into the cloud and there you find your favorite blanket . . . umm . . . it feels so good to cuddle up with it . . . how good and comfortable this feels . . . so comfortable that you gently rest . . . so happy and relaxed . . . sleep peacefully through the night . . . and awaken in the morning feeling bright, rested, and cheerful.

In the example above, it isn't necessary to do a closing since the child will be falling asleep. We can adapt a journey like this one to relate to specifics in children's lives. If they have a dog, use its name. If there is another pet that the children love, such as a cat, let the cat appear in the story. Find on the cloud things that children love the most, such as a favorite stuffed animal or doll. Use images that children can relate to, and keep it simple. A lot of imagery is not necessary.

This next journey helps children find a special inner place. This is a safe space that they can visit to relax, to ease tension when they are upset, to get an answer to a question or problem, or to get into a relaxed state of mind. Again, adapt this generic journey to suit the children's needs. Younger children can go to a place that they like, while upper-elementary-age children might meet an inner heroine. Remember to have children get into comfortable, relaxed positions. Then go ahead and coach them through this journey.

A Special Inner Place

Relax . . . breathe deeply . . . breathing in . . . and out . . . and with each breath we notice that we are becoming more and more relaxed. Notice your toes . . . wiggle them and then just let them relax . . . feel the feet relax . . . your legs are letting go of all tension . . . relax your back . . . breathe into your stomach and just let all of your muscles relax . . . it's as if we are melting into the floor . . . breathe deeply, and as you let the breath go . . . relax your chest . . . and your shoulders . . . with each breath we are becoming . . . more and more relaxed . . . letting go of tension in your arms . . . hands . . . fingers . . . relaxing your neck . . . cheeks . . . eyes . . . forehead . . . becoming totally relaxed and comfortable. . . .

Now picture yourself walking through a path in the woods. See the sun glimmering through the trees . . . hear a brook bubbling by . . . smell the pine trees that surround you . . . ahh . . . what a beautiful day . . . continue along the path, which leads you to a doorway . . . you know that this doorway leads you to a special place . . . a place that is all your own . . . where you feel good . . . notice the door . . . touch it . . . What is it made of? . . . What is its texture? . . . What color is it? . . . Are there any symbols on it? . . . Open the door and step inside to a special quiet space . . . in this space you feel so calm . . . look around . . . What do you see? . . . Are there any sounds in this private special place? . . . Are there any smells in the air? . . . What are you standing or sitting on? . . . Your heart soars at the comfort the special place brings you . . . it is so peaceful here . . . you feel safe and happy . . . stay in your space for a while.

[We may choose whether to include the next section. If not, go to the "Closing" section below.]

In your safe space, you can get answers to questions that you
may have . . . your inner guidance is available at any time . . . see
your inner guide or inner hero . . . What does this guide look like?
. . . Is there a message for you? . . . An answer to a question you
may have? . . . Your guide has a gift for you . . . receive it now . . .
stay with your special friend for a while.

[Closing:] *And now, prepare to return from the journey . . .*
remembering all that has happened in your special space . . . and
knowing this is a special space that you can return to at any time
. . . you go back through the door . . . walk along the path . . .
carrying with you the calm and clear feelings you found in your
special space . . . feel alert and . . . refreshed.

A good follow-up activity to this particular journey is to have the children draw or paint a picture of the special inner place. It might be a tree house, a sunny spot in the bedroom that they like, or a scene high on a mountain. Remember that there is no right or wrong in the imagery. This is the child's space, and we honor it.

Having our children express their inner journeys artistically provides an opportunity to share their mind's images in the physical world. To help them remember the journey, we can ask questions:

- ☞ Did they see symbols on the door? *Ask them to draw the door.*
- ☞ Did they meet up with an inner heroine? *Have them draw a picture of this meeting or hero.*
- ☞ Were they given any messages or gifts? *If we don't have the children meet with an inner guide, we might have them find a gift in*

their special inner space. Again, modify the journey to fit the needs of the children.

These sample journeys are merely guidelines. We are the coaches for our children's creativity, so modify these exercises for various ages and outcomes. Just remember that children relate best to images and places that are comfortable, safe, and familiar to them.

Using Guided Stories for Specific Situations

Physical and Emotional Relief

When children are sick, we can use guided imagery to help them relax and be more comfortable. We might suggest that they imagine themselves talking with the part of their body that hurts to see what it needs. Have them picture what the disease or pain looks like and then what it would look like if they were feeling healthy. Or have them befriend the sickness. They can send healing energy or rainbow colors into the part of them that doesn't feel well. One little boy used to visualize Pac-Man eating up his cancer cells. It lifted his feelings of powerlessness and helped him feel that he was participating in his own healing.

Remember, if the mind believes the body is getting better, the mindbody relationship promotes healing. In turn, the body can give messages back to the mind, such as having the sickness give an image or a gift to the children in the process of the journey.

Special Challenges

Use guided imagery to help children prepare for upcoming challenges such as a sporting event. In the journey, coach her to see herself doing very well during the event and succeeding. Have her feel her confidence. Let her see herself in the midst of the commotion of other competitors and screaming crowds. Remember to incorporate as many of the senses as possible: What does the air smell like? Can you hear your breathing? Can you hear the other runners breathing next to you? Listen to the crowd clapping. Feel your pulse. Imagine what it feels like to reach your goal.

Schoolwork

Use guided imagery to help your child with schoolwork. For instance, if he's studying the ocean, guide him through an undersea journey. Have him visualize various ocean animals, plants, and images. Or, if he's learning the alphabet, in one journey we might have him picture things that begin with the letter A. In another, move on to the letter B. Coach him to imagine reading with ease or easily grasping new mathematical concepts. Encourage him to believe he can do it.

Family Relationships

Use guided imagery to solve family problems. Children can visualize being able to share their toys and belongings with their siblings. In groups of children who had been routinely coached through guided journeys, there was more compassion and acceptance among them. They began to use positive language and statements such as, "I listen well," "I can do it," and "I am special." Overall, they seemed to show a more caring attitude toward one another.

There are many ways in which to incorporate guided imagery into our children's world. This simple yet powerful tool is a gift they can carry with them throughout their lives.

10

Breath: The Single Most Important Exercise
You Can Teach Your Children

With time, we may notice that our way of
breathing perfectly reflects our way of life.
Michael Sky

How you breathe reflects your self-esteem. How you breathe directly correlates to your enjoyment and satisfaction in life. These are startling statements, yet we can observe their truth in those around us.

If you breathe deeply, you imbibe of life and what it has to offer. If you are a shallow breather, perhaps you are not confident and feeling safe.

I interviewed first graders and, with the teachers, analyzed their breathing. Only one child breathed deeply. All the other first graders were already shallow breathers by age six. How do you think they felt starting first grade as shallow breathers—eager, confident, and safe, or anxious, stressed, and fearful?

Experts agree that shallow, chest breathing is associated with anxiety, high blood pressure, nervous disorders, depression, and psychosomatic disorders.

► *Deep breathing, using the diaphragm muscle and belly, quiets the mind, reduces blood pressure, uplifts unhealthy attitudes, and decreases psychosomatic symptoms.*

Encourage children to breathe more effectively so they can become

- Internally healthy in a polluted environment
- Emotionally secure and able to control their emotions
- Able to mentally focus on their schoolwork and hobbies
- Open and caring in their attitude toward life

► *It is mandatory that we teach children effective breathing for their health and life success.*

In this chapter we emphasize diaphragmatic breathing—taking deeper and fuller breaths into the abdominal area. The purpose of this *more effective* breathing technique is to

- Bring more oxygen into the body
- Activate the relaxation response
- Exercise the breathing muscles
- Revitalize the body's energy

Breathwork and breath therapies are to the next millennium's children what physical fitness has been to the children of the past four decades. The '60s made us aware that we needed to move and exercise our bodies in order to feel better. The last two decades have brought about a revolution in the way we think about our diets and nutrition. But if our bodies are not taking in and using oxygen effectively, then our health is not complete.

► *Teaching children how to bring awareness to their breath and to control their breathing patterns is the easiest, cheapest, and most naturally effective way to encourage self-control, empowerment, and a healthy body.*

However, because breathing is also an involuntary act, children may not always understand the benefits and the need of deeper breathing. This chapter explores the power of aware breathing and ways to achieve it.

► *Children can learn to use the breath as a tool to safely integrate their feelings and emotions, increase skill levels, and stay mentally focused.*

Children have a natural interest in their breath and often play with it, holding it in and blowing it out to see what happens. Coaching children to breathe by breathing with them shows them how to relax and enjoy the process. We always want breathing activities to be fun and to be associated with openness and playfulness.

So introducing breathing techniques in a playful atmosphere encourages children to use them on their own and with a healthy attitude toward their benefits. This is what a group of six-year-old children told me about their breathing activities in the classroom:

"I'm nicer."

"I feel gooder."

"I'm happier, but I don't know why."

"I just like it, that's all."

EFFECTIVE BREATHING

Do we breathe effectively? In most cases, no! Think of the breath as the fuel for our inner fire and the breathing mechanism as a carburetor for our engine. For optimum health, we want to keep our engine parts clean and our lungs free from pollutants. When we breathe deeper and fuller, we are not only taking in the oxygen necessary for life, we are cleansing our bodies as well. When we exhale, we release carbon dioxide, tension, and stress. Studies indicate that over 70 percent of our body's toxins are released through the breath.

Jack Shields, M.D., a lymphologist from Santa Barbara, California, conducted a study on the effects of breathing on the lymphatic system. Using cameras inside the body, he found that deep, diaphragmatic breathing stimulates the cleansing of the lymph system by creating a vacuum effect which sucks the lymph through the bloodstream. This increases the rate of toxic elimination by as much as fifteen times the normal rate.[1]

▶ *Every time we breathe consciously, we ask for more of the richness and rewards that life offers.*

At the turn of the last century, people spoke of "taking in the air." The idea was to go outdoors, breathe deeply, and open the nasal passages to the odors borne on the wind. In fact, this practice has great benefits for the body. Dilating the nostrils and closing the eyes gently stimulates the nervous system and relaxes the body.

REFLECTIONS

Visualize in your mind that you're pulling tiny energy bubbles from the air through your nostrils and into your lungs and that this flow circulates throughout your body, energizing and revitalizing you.

OXYGEN IS A KEY TO HEALTH

The purpose of breathing is not merely to move air but also to move energy.[2] Breathing is the primary way in which humans convert energy into physical form. Oxygen plays a vital role in the chemical reactions inside the body, from releasing cellular energy to fueling our organs.

The body cannot store more than a few minutes of oxygen. A continual supply passes through the lungs almost directly into the blood for circulation. Because every cell needs energy, oxygen is the main component triggering chemical reactions for the cell to release energy. Carbon dioxide is the waste product.

The average oxygen concentration in the blood is between 60 and 70 percent. The minimal life-sustaining percentage is 53 percent. Above 80 percent, oxygen saturation in the blood acts as a tremendous boost to health, vitality, and the ability of the body to detoxify. The way to increase oxygen is to breathe deeper and fuller. If we wish to restore balance and harmony, it is important to breathe in the most effective way.

▶ *Just by observing how we breathe, we actually change our breath pattern.*

Respiration is slightly different from the other physiological functions of the body. While it is a self-governing activity, we can easily influence it by bringing our awareness to the breath. By observing our breathing, we automatically deepen and slow its pace to produce calm.

People who breathe slowly and deeply are confident, emotionally stable, and physically and intellectually active.[3] On the other hand, improper breathing habits can cause "cardiac

157

symptoms, angina, respiratory symptoms, gastrointestinal distress, anxiety, panic, depression, headache, dizziness, seizures, increased susceptibility to infection and other immune system dysfunction, sleep disturbances. . . ."[4]

When our children present symptoms of stress, anxiety, fear, or discomfort, breathing is the first place, not the last, that we should look for disordered energy. We are most likely to observe a shallow breathing effect, causing a high chest, raised shoulders, and tight solar plexus and diaphragm.

WHY IS OUR BREATHING RESTRICTED?

If you were born in the United States, your first deep breath was probably accompanied by a sharp slap on your rear. That was enough for many of us to become shallow breathers from the start! Yet when we observe the natural breathing of newborn children, we notice that their bellies are gently rounded and relaxed and that they breathe continuously without a pause between the inhale and exhale. This so-called *circular breathing* is a very healthy way to breathe.

If circular breathing and consciously directing our breath are so good for us, why aren't more of us doing it? Why do we breathe using our chest muscles instead of the deeper, more natural way? The answer is simple, and we observe it every day.

As children, we often became overwhelmed by our feelings. *We discovered, as children, that if we held our breath and stiffened our diaphragms, we wouldn't feel our emotions.* This created a false sense of safety and set us up for a lifetime of restricted breathing whenever we were faced with intense emotions.

When we change our own restricted breath patterns and use circular breathing, we will feel our feelings. Coaching our children in the same technique can help them feel safe with their emotions and supply them with a tool they can use to calm themselves and feel peaceful.

A second obstacle to healthy breathing is our culture's emphasis on body image. The thin-waist syndrome imposed by this culture on both genders causes us to pull the abdomen in and push the chest out. This limits the movement of the diaphragm muscle and increases chest breathing.

Another major barrier to effective breathing is stress! In our busy lives, we tend to isolate our breathing to the chest area. When this happens, the sympathetic nervous system believes there is a crisis and prepares us for "fight or flight." Chest breathing also creates chronic tension in the abdominal and chest muscles and can lead to difficulties with digestion. By consciously changing our breathing patterns, we can easily break this disabling habit in our own bodies and keep our children from ever developing it.

REFLECTIONS

Take a moment now to observe your own breath pattern and analyze your patterns based on these questions: Does the breath begin in the belly and roll up through the chest? Do you breathe continuously or do you stop and start? Are you a deep breather or a shallow breather? Does your breath start in the chest or throat? Do you find yourself holding your breath when you are concentrating or in a tense situation?

The average adult and most older children breathe in stops and starts, mostly from the chest instead of the diaphragm. Younger children, on the other hand, are natural belly breathers. Therefore, when we see them breathing from the chest, it's usually a sign of tension or anxiety. When children seem to be enjoying life the most, their breath is full and continuous.

When we stop breathing deeply, we tense so as not to feel the rising emotions. We operate solely from our unconscious habits and programming. We react to our world instead of being balanced and responsive within it.

Tension, frozen feelings, trauma, and emotional reactions cause us to feel separated from the flow of life. Conscious breathing restores our balance so that we can be in a state of response, feeling fluid and connected. We can then stop worrying about the future and the past and focus more directly on being present with our family.

What Is an Effective Breath?

A healthy breath begins in the abdomen and rises gently into the chest. All of the emphasis is on the inhale, drawing in. The exhale, a gentle letting-go, requires no effort. A simple sigh at the end signals completed cycles of inhale and exhale.

▶ *Inhale, filling the belly like a balloon, and relax as the air makes a whooshing sound as the diaphragm contracts, expelling air from the lungs.*

Typically, we breathe through the nostrils. Tiny hairs inside the nose filter dust so it doesn't reach the lungs. Breathing through the nose also moistens and warms the air for us. There are both therapeutic and martial-arts approaches to breathing that use mouth breathing. For our purposes, we suggest nostril breathing unless otherwise indicated. But when faced with an emotionally charged situation, breathing with an open mouth maximizes the intake of oxygen and brings balance to the situation more quickly.

CIRCULAR BREATHING

Place the palm of your hand on your abdomen so that you can feel your belly expand with air as you inhale and roll your breath up into your chest. At the top of the inhale, relax and release your breath completely with a gentle sigh. Repeat this several times, breathing in an easy, continuous cycle. It is so easy!

Notice how your body automatically relaxes and your mind feels clearer. This simple exercise in circular breathing energizes the body by bringing oxygen to the bloodstream and releasing tension and stress. When we breathe rhythmically and deeply, fully and easily, we issue an inner command for the brain to slow down. Patterns of stress held in the body automatically dissipate, and the body relaxes. The brain slows to the rate at which intuition operates. The mindbody system becomes peaceful. Continuing this breathing for several minutes brings us to deeper states of physical relaxation, emotional calm, and mental focus.

By consciously breathing, we can

- Produce a relaxed brain wave state
- Soothe our bodily tension
- Heighten our awareness at will
- Sense and feel clearly through our bodies what is going on

☞ Connect more fully with our environment and with people

☞ Feel calm, balanced, and in control

Breathing in a conscious, connected pattern is fun, safe, easy, and free. By making conscious breathing a family activity, all of us can experience its benefits.

OBSERVE YOUR BREATHING

Now let's observe our own breathing more closely. Lie down and breathe in the normal pattern that is comfortable for you. Watch which part of the body rises on the inhale. The chest? The stomach? The belly? The shoulders? The lower we breathe on each inhale, the better we are doing.

If the inspiration lifts our chest, lungs, and heart area, consider the anxiety associated with our shallow breathing patterns. Based on what research has shown us, the more shallow the breath, the less oxygen we're receiving. The deeper, the better!

REFLECTIONS

Watch how you breathe. Do you use the diaphragm? (The diaphragm is the elongated muscle under the rib cage that extends around to the back and moves the abdominal muscles.) Do you breathe in short gasps or sighs? Do you tend to prefer the nose or the mouth? Remember, the deeper, the better.

Here is an opportunity for the whole family to relearn appropriate breathing patterns. Begin by practicing the following breathing technique on yourself. It is necessary for balance, harmony, and health.

DEEP BELLY BREATHING

Place your hand on your belly. As you inhale, push the belly outward or upward. This may take some practice, as most people in Western culture are shallow breathers. Breathe in long, slow, and deep breaths, making the belly rise. On the exhale, sigh and release gently. Don't prolong the exhale. Then take the next breath immediately. Don't pause or hold the breath for extended time periods.

The goal is to connect one breath to another. The continuous stream of inhale and exhale expands and relaxes the body and mind and brings a continuous supply of oxygen to both. This automatically means a healthier body and a clear mind.

Now try this process with your children. Ask them to lie down. Observe their breathing patterns, and guide them into the breathing technique we have practiced. In most cases, children tend to imitate what they have learned from their parents. Sometimes children are avid in their desire to do it right. They breathe enthusiastically and work up a rhythm as if they were dancing. When you teach your children the deep belly breathing, emphasize the relaxed pace and gentle rhythm. There is no rush, and each person will find their own pace of breathing for their own comfort.

LEARNING THROUGH OBSERVATION

Teach the use of breathing techniques through concrete and tangible suggestions that engage the five senses and make awareness exercises fun. It is often easier for children to watch others, both adults and peers, breathe before becoming aware of their own breathing patterns. They can observe and ask

- ☞ Where in their bodies do people breathe?
- ☞ How do people breathe?
- ☞ Why would people want to breathe better
- ☞ How could they do so?

This works best if the children can first observe someone lying down. As the person inhales, the children watch which three parts of the body fall or rise—chest, diaphragm, or belly.

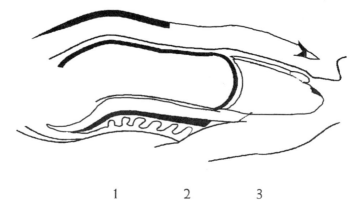

| 1 | 2 | 3 |

During the Easter holiday, one parent who is certified in the TransformBreathing™ process kept her six-year-old daughter entertained by playing the game Breath Doctor. They engaged various relatives to be diagnosed by the doctor.

Elsabet was very creative in her play. She used her toy stethoscope to listen to the quality of breath in the lungs as each person breathed. She asked them to cough. She asked them to lie down and breathe so she could see where they expanded with air. She told two chest-breathing relatives that they should breathe lower. She carried a clipboard with paper and drew pictures for the family members of what their breath looked like.

THE "WHERE" AND "HOW" OF BREATHING

As we teach children to observe *where* people breathe, we can also help them to observe the *how* of breathing. The following questions tell children what to look for.

- Do you hold your breath?
- Is breathing hard or easy?
- How do you inhale? Smooth, jerky, flowing, catching, deep, or shallow?
- What words would you use to describe your inhale?
- How do you exhale? Long, short, deep, shallow, catching, or smoothly?
- What words would you use to describe your exhale?
- Does it feel good to breathe? If not, what word would describe it?
- How do you breathe when you sit?
- How do you breathe when you stand? When you lie down?
- How is breathing in those positions alike or different?
- How do you breathe when you walk?
- How do breathe when you run?
- How is breathing different when you move than when you're still, like sitting?

165

Once children have mastered observing the breath of others, they will know what to look for in themselves. They can observe their own breath while lying down in front of a mirror to watch themselves. As they inhale, instruct them to place their hand on whichever body part rises. As they exhale, have them describe it to you using as concrete descriptors as possible. This exercise teaches breath awareness.

As we are teaching children to be aware of their breath, we can emphasize how important deep breathing is by using such statements as

☞ "Good, we know where your breath is, and eventually we'll get it all the way down to here (pointing to the lower abdomen)."

☞ "That's a wonderful breath, and I bet you can go even deeper."

☞ "Explain to me where you think the breath is."

BREATHING WITH INFANTS

From the moment our infants are born, we can breathe with them. The best way to do this is to simply hold them close to our body in any position that is comfortable for both of us and begin breathing deeply and rhythmically. This can be done sitting in a comfortable chair or standing. In my experience, many infants seem to prefer that we stand. Experiment to find what works best. After a few minutes of breathing, the baby's breath will often match our own pace. This is very soothing and relaxing for both participants.

BREATHING WITH TODDLERS AND YOUNG CHILDREN

Children ages three and under are very busy. As far as they're concerned, they have places to go and people to see, so please don't interfere. The best time to introduce breathing practice is at naptime or just before going to bed so children associate breathing with relaxation.

Toddlers

Place your hand on the child's belly, encouraging her to breathe into the belly and lift up the hand as she does so. Breathe deeply and rhythmically so children can hear. Soft, soothing music in the background provides a gentle rhythm to help children breathe. Dr. Tom Goode's *Cosmic Waltz* was designed for breathing rhythms and practice.[5] We can introduce the idea of a "happy belly." Children realize that when their belly is open and relaxed, they feel good.

Making silly faces and being dramatic with breath is also appealing to this age group. We can pretend that we are balloons and take three deep breaths to fill ourselves up. Hold the third breath, and then while exhaling make a loud *"Aahhh"* sound. Slump over to demonstrate that all the air is out of our balloon, and then smile and sit up as the balloon is filled again.

In their zest for life, children of this age incur a lot of knocks and bruises. When the tears flow, all we need do is scoop up our child, hold him against our belly and heart, and breathe deeply with an open mouth. Children quickly learn to associate the breath with feeling better faster so they can get back to business. No words are needed. The breath says it all!

Ages Six to Nine

For children ages six to nine, the techniques described for the under-five groups also work well. In addition, we can explain to them how they can do this for themselves and what's in it for them—such as feeling good about themselves and enjoying life. This age group is becoming involved in activities away from their parents, which can create occasional anxiety and fear.

▶ *They are old enough to understand that when they're upset or scared, they can breathe deeply in their bellies and they will quickly feel better.*

Some children this age feel they're getting too big to sit on a lap when they're hurt. We can still pull them in close to us and breathe until their attention has shifted and they feel more peaceful.

One friend was amazed by the transformative power of breath in her own life and wanted to share it with her six-year-old son, who'd had asthma since he was two. She wanted to introduce the process gradually. Every night after her son was asleep she sat next to his bed and started her circular-breathing pattern. She soon found that the family dog joined her, breathing in and out in the same rhythm. Her sleeping son's breathing quickly began to follow the same pattern. Her son has experienced less severe and less frequent asthma attack since she began her nighttime breathing sessions with him.

As always, when we teach these techniques, we must meet our children where they are. If we are sharing circular breathing and children laugh, then we can laugh and smile. If the child curls up in a fetal position or does not respond, gently touch her while continuing to breathe. Observe the child's reaction, because she will share with you nonverbally how she wants to learn.

When Tom first taught his eight-year-old stepdaughter, Kristen, circular breathing, all she did was giggle. When she giggled, Tom took his cue to use laughter. On the exhale, they used a *Ha!-aah!*

sound and smiled at each other. Tom and Kristen inhaled together, and smiled again. Without a pause in their breathing pattern, they exhaled dramatically, saying, *"Ha!-aah!"* Later they clapped their hands and stamped their feet to the *"Ha!-aah!"*

When Tom smiled at Kristen, she knew that he wasn't judging her breathing as right or wrong. When he made the sound with her, she knew that it was a game they were playing to teach her something new. Dramatizing with sound and movement was fun to her. Afterward, Tom discussed with Kristen how this breath pattern might help her to stop and clear her mind to think clearly or relieve stress, particularly at school. By the time they got around to their discussion, it was two friends talking with each other, not a stepfather lecturing a child.

Ages Nine and Up

Many children are now involved in sports, recitals, or testing at school. Before any event they can sit, calm themselves, and start breathing deeply and rhythmically. They can imagine themselves in the upcoming situation and feel themselves as successful, confident, and happily achieving their goal.

If they keep their breath open during the event, they will be more relaxed and able to maintain their focus. Even though children of this age group are very independent and may appear at times to be mature, many of the techniques from the six-to-nine group still work well. They will see that they can use the breath to clear their minds, relax, relieve their own stress, and meet their personal achievement goals.

▶ *Children ages nine and up can utilize the dynamic power of visualization, imagery, and breath to create the results they want in their lives.*

169

IMAGERY AND BREATH

Beginning with toddlers, you can also use guided imagery or stories with the breath. Here's an example of a calming visualization that combines imagery and breath.

> *Children can sit or lie down in a comfortable position. Ask them*
> *to close their eyes and imagine they are floating on puffy white*
> *clouds. Have them breathe in slowly through their nose while*
> *saying to themselves in their mind, "I am peaceful." And then*
> *have them exhale while mentally repeating, "I am calm,"*
> *and imagining they are riding on the white cloud. Repeat*
> *this several times. Play soft music in the background to*
> *enhance the effect.*

PUTTING IT ALL TOGETHER

There is a lot of blending and overlapping among the techniques we use for the different age groups. There are no hard and fast distinctions. We can be flexible and follow our own creativity and intuition. As we use these simple breathing techniques, we'll find that our awareness becomes clearer.

We know our child best. We know the mental images that make her smile. We have the memories of peaceful places that can create the warm fuzzy feelings. We can lovingly share any memories we know our children would enjoy while they are focusing on circular, diaphragmatic breathing.

EMOTIONAL INTEGRATION

Newborns begin life using fuller and deeper breathing naturally. Their bellies gently rise and fall as they inhale and exhale without a pause. Holding their breath is learned later in life during moments of trauma and intense emotion. This sets us up for a lifetime of restricted breathing patterns. *When we stop breathing, even for a short time, our body becomes tense, our feelings shut down, and our mind rushes in to take control.* We then react to our world instead of being balanced and responsive within it. And we can prevent this. We can use the relaxed, full breath to reverse this process and coach our children in the same life skill.

Studies by International Breath Institute facilitators who work with the TransformBreathing™ process show that circular breathing can help integrate feelings. This breathing technique activates repressed energy patterns and the suppressed emotion is then experienced in the body. There may be tears, laughter, or anger as the old emotions rise to the surface. While we don't usually recall the exact memory of the event, we can feel the integrated energy in the body as a twitching, tingling, numbness, or fluttering in the muscles. Afterward we often feel lighter and elated and, most of all, connected to the whole of life again.

In adults, the repressed patterns usually come from old emotions associated with family dysfunction, including physical and psychological abuse. With children, the suppressed emotions may be connected with unpleasant experiences such as disappointment, resentment, anger, and fear that have been forgotten at the conscious level. As long as these emotions remain in the subconscious mind, though, they will continue to affect our day-to-day lives. Unless resolved and integrated, these emotions can surprise us at any time, causing us to overreact inappropriately.

The good news is that we can integrate our stuck emotions now! Moreover, we can coach our children to keep their own emotions flowing freely by teaching them circular, deeper breathing. This coaching can be easily incorporated into your life. You're probably already using many of the techniques naturally. Now you can use them consciously and expand on them.

▶ *Simple breathing techniques can be used for both stress relief and family bonding.*

One evening a mother watched her daughter playing dodgeball with the neighbors on our front lawn. In the excitement of the game, a boy threw the ball too hard. The impact knocked the daughter down. She was more surprised than angry and more shocked than hurt. Her breathing immediately became panting, as if she were trying to catch her breath. Her mouth opened and heaving movements started in her chest. Her adrenaline was pumping, and she was becoming angry. What she did next surprised the mother. Instead of wanting to hit or yell at the little boy, she lay down on the ground. The mother had taught her daughter to do this on a camping trip once. The daughter closed her eyes and took several deep breaths. She later told her mother that she was too hurt and confused to get up and was embarrassed when she was knocked down. She remembered the camping trip advice: "If you don't know what to do when something is wrong, just close your eyes, take several deep breaths, and count to ten."

PEER RELATIONSHIPS
Teaching children appropriate breathing shows them how to safely integrate their feelings, increase their skill levels,

and stay mentally focused on their schoolwork. Diane Stein, a TransformBreathing™ trainer from Durango, Colorado, has found breath a natural and effective way to help her daughter through the inevitable challenges of peer relationships:

> *I breathe with my daughter when she has problems with other kids at school. For example, one little girl was picking on her and getting the other girls in the class to gang up on her. She came home upset day after day.*
>
> *Finally, we breathed with the intention of sending the other little girl some love. The breathing session helped my daughter shift the way she responded to the little girl, and she didn't get upset anymore. Later, they became the best of friends.*
>
> *Now when my daughter comes home from school, I use breath with her to help her refocus. She likes me to pay attention to her. Sometimes it only takes ten minutes, but it's a focused time when she and I can be together completely in a positive and loving way with no distractions.*

When we breathe rhythmically and deeply, fully and easily, we issue an inner command for the brain to slow down. Stress in the body dissipates automatically, and the body relaxes. We feel calm, balanced, and in control. Appropriate breathing is how we can help our children respond to life in joy. "In using breath with my fourteen-year-old daughter, I find that we transform patterns of irritation between us," explains Cynthia Campbell of Asheville, North Carolina. "Our heart bond is always much stronger after we breathe."

FAMILY DYNAMICS

Jill Leigh of Portland, Maine, uses breath to help shift the patterns of interaction within her family. She says,

> *I am a high-powered sales consultant earning a six-figure income in the work world. I have scheduled a TransformBreathing™ facilitator to come in to work with my family. It's about helping me to make a transition to more effective mothering by giving my son, Andrew, literally the space to breathe without my controlling personality. I know I am overprotective and controlling in the family setting, and I run a lot of guilt about "Am I a good mother?" because I don't do those traditional motherly things, like reading to him. Sometimes I don't have patience when he's doing simple, eight-year-old stuff.*
>
> *Breathing is the key to the larger connection for my family. My husband wants to breathe to deal with his stress. I don't parent with finesse so I am working on the balance between my inner male and female. I encourage Andrew to work on his asthma through breath and develop a skill set he can use the rest of his life. He may not have the language and the syntax to understand how we deal with family issues. And he doesn't have to. Andrew will learn that TransformBreathing™ is the base of our family structure and dynamics. He'll know it's a tool we use to communicate and bond together.*

Like Leigh, parents can help their children by breathing with them before emotions become stuck or frozen in the body as restricted breathing patterns. As parents, we can also benefit from what we are teaching our children. We all need a quick way to break through our stressful emotions to a place of calm. Make conscious breathing a family activity and everybody benefits. By doing so, you'll emphasize the value of the individuals and your relationship to them.

BREATHING EXERCISES

The following exercises work well for the whole family and may even set a new trend in party games.

The Bird

Like a bird preparing for flight, this exercise helps build energy and release tension. It is good to use when you want more energy and a sharper mental focus.

1. Standing, with knees bent, raise your arms overhead while inhaling.
2. Exhaling, bring your arms down to shoulder level.
3. Inhale and repeat for two to five minutes.
4. Release the breath, close your eyes, and bring your awareness to the sensation of energy in your body.

This exercise is more effective when we breathe with our mouths open and remember to breathe deeply into our bellies on the inhale. Play any upbeat, bouncy music you like to make it even more fun. This exercise is a wonderful prelude to studying or to any activity in which we need to concentrate and focus our mind. It's also a good way for us, as adults, to start our day by energizing our entire system.

The Tree

A tree will grow tall only if its roots go deep into the earth. Your legs form the roots of the tree; your spine is the trunk; your arms the branches.

1. Stand up straight with your feet parallel and slightly apart. Keep your shoulders relaxed and down, the back of your neck long, and your chin slightly tucked in.
2. Keep your left leg straight. Breathe out, take your right foot, and place it high on the inside of your left thigh.
3. Your weight should be on the heel of the standing foot, which goes down into the ground like a tree root. Relax your shoulders and put the palms of your hands together.
4. Inhaling, slowly raise your arms above your head like tree branches. Exhaling, come down and repeat the pose standing on your right leg and raising your left foot.

This exercise assists us in feeling grounded. It alleviates that "spacey" feeling. We find and feel our natural state of balance and focus.

The Lion

This is a fun exercise for relieving pent-up energy and gently stretching and strengthening the body. If your child is feeling frustrated about a situation and not ready to talk about it, this often releases enough energy so that he can share his feelings.

For very young children this gives an appropriate way to express their physical energy. The breath integrates their feelings so they don't need to act them out.

1. Standing tall and balanced with your arms by your sides, take a deep breath, drawing it into your entire body. Repeat as often as desired.
2. Exhaling with a growl sound, lunge your right foot forward with arms and hands coming out in front of you in a cat attack position. Hamming up facial expressions is fun.
3. Inhaling, come back to your original upright position.
4. Repeat, alternating the leg that lunges forward.

Focused inhaling helps our children and us to greater self-awareness. Realize that as you become a breath coach, you're sharing with your children life-enhancing tools that will always be with them. These tools will assist them to feel self-confident, inspire them to dream, and then empower them to live those dreams.

11

Music Magic

Music washes away from the soul the dust of everyday life.
Red Auerbach

Music speaks to our emotions and opens the door to our hearts. It calms our mind, relaxes our bodies, and reunites us with our innermost desires and dreams. It can bypass our conscious mind and allow us to enter the nonconscious realm where we can express our feelings. Beethoven has referred to music as "the mediator between the life of the senses and the life of the spirit."[1] It is one of the gateways to our dreams and the unfolding of children's gifts.

▶ *Sound, rhythm, and music are tools that can help our children express and release emotions and learn to cooperate and listen. Most importantly, they can be keys that activate their dream.*

Because music has such a strong effect on all of us, children learn how vibrations and rhythms affect their moods and energy levels and how to use that effect to their advantage. This chapter offers exercises that teach children how to use their heartbeat to restore balance, how to transform their moods through music, and how to use sound and vibration to relax. There are exercises we can use one-on-one with a child and other activities that involve the entire family. As our children bang on drums, hum humorous songs, and mimic natural sounds, they discover the joy and transformative powers of music.

THE POWER OF MUSIC

Listening to music yields powerful, tangible results. It can increase vitality and relieve fatigue as well as uplift and balance moodiness. Music helps to focus the mind and inspire creativity.

Like conscious breathing, music is one of the most powerful stress reducers there is. Countless studies have shown the physiological benefits gained from listening to enjoyable music. Plants exposed to classical music grow larger and give higher yields than plants without this stimulus.

Just like plants and animals, our audible environment affects us. We live in a world that is constantly pulling us out of our natural rhythm. Science calls this *stress*. We even use musical terms to describe how we feel: "out-of-synch," "tuned out," or "out-of-harmony" with our body and our environment. In our high-tech, fast-paced world, our senses are constantly bombarded with a variety of sounds, rhythms, and machine vibrations that cause our body to shift into different—often unnatural—rhythms throughout the day. Music brings us back.

Music using certain types of rhythm does bring about a state of relaxed alertness and physical calm. It is the predominantly alpha brain-wave pattern that psychological researchers find is often associated with meditation. Music can do in minutes what we might strive for in weeks of meditative practice.

The tempo of music will slow our heartbeat, lower blood pressure, and reduce stress hormones in the blood, in some cases replacing the need for medication.[2] Listening to half an hour of classical music produces the same effect as ten milligrams of Valium for hospitalized heart patients.[3]

Music has power over our physiology and psychology because music *bypasses* our mental processes. We can't "think" the vibration of music out of our body. Even when our minds ignore or don't actively listen to music, the sounds and vibrations still enter our body subconsciously. As our heartbeat, pulse, breathing, and nervous system absorb the vibrations, the music affects us by calming us or exciting us or moving us to tears. Music can make us dance.

Music with a strong drumbeat has a powerful effect on our internal body rhythms. In aboriginal cultures, the drumbeat represents and mimics the human heartbeat; this is an important part of the healing tradition of many cultures. As music itself is a combination of different rhythms, so too is our heartbeat. It consists of a contraction, called the *systole*, and a relaxation, called the *diastole*. These two actions are controlled by the sympathetic and parasympathetic nervous systems, both of which are influenced by sound waves and music.

MUSIC IN CHILDHOOD

Love, respect, and appreciation for music are easy to share with our children. During the first few years of our child's life, we can teach basic musical skills that build self-esteem and enhance self-expression. Musical rhythms spur motor development in children. Learning melodies and words stimulates children's capacity to listen and develop receptive language. Many areas of child development and learning are positively affected by exposure to and training in music. Preschoolers given piano and voice lessons, for example, have been found to improve dramatically in their ability to put together picture puzzles of animals. Playing the piano at the preschool age influences the brain during development of the cortex, the part of the brain that is used for thinking, talking, seeing, hearing, and creating.[4] Music training has also been shown to contribute to the ability to learn or enhance mathematics skills.

Music clearly is a resource for living, growing, and learning that we, as aware parents, will want to make part of our children's experience, especially to cultivate dreaming.

EXPLORING SOUND, RHYTHM, MELODY, AND MUSIC

Another way to explain music is to break it down into its three basic components.:

$$Sound + Rhythm + Melody = Music$$

Sound

To help children understand music, it is helpful to look at each component separately. First there is sound. It can be a sound that we make or one that is made from another source. A few examples of sound are a bird chirping, a teakettle whistling, and a child banging on a pot with a spoon. If music were compared to a painting, sound would be the background color. In our bodies, sound corresponds with our central nervous system. A pleasant sound opens and expands us. It can energize or calm us. A shrieking sound will cause us to contract. Like the background in a painting, sound is the first step in creating music.

Here are some ways to explore sound with our children:

- Have your children listen to the sounds around them. How many different sounds can they find in the kitchen or backyard?
- Encourage children to be creative making sounds. Have them use their voices or household objects to make sound. Allow them to make pretty, irritating, or silly sounds. All sounds are music if they reflect creative exploration or honest feelings.

The purpose for creating sound is not necessarily to make "beautiful music" but to foster self-expression and open up our children's ears to the world around them.

Rhythm

The second component of music is rhythm. Rhythm gives sound the beat, providing and organizing it. For example, is the whistling of the teakettle long and steady or short and choppy? Is the child's banging on the pot fast and upbeat or smooth and slow? In a painting, the rhythm would be the overall movement or flow of the composition. When you first look at the painting, where do your eyes go? Is the painting easy to look at or is it busy and annoying? This is its rhythm.

In our bodies, rhythm corresponds to our own internal body rhythm—our pulse and breath. If the musical beat is quick and steady, our heartbeat and body movements will start to mirror it. If we are tired, listening to African drumming can kick our body back into gear. On the other hand, if a two-year-old is running around out of control, slow rhythmic music like Bach or Vivaldi restores inner calm and slows most children down. Explore and add rhythm to the sounds that children make.

- ☞ Have your children play with different beats: fast, slow, steady, and erratic.
- ☞ Have them practice listening to the different rhythms around them, like the water dripping from the faucet or the ticking of a clock.
- ☞ Ask them if they can feel the vibration of a musical beat in their bodies, and if so, where? How do the different rhythms feel in their body? How do their feet want to move with the different beats?
- ☞ Try hand clapping to the rhythm of a poem and foot tapping to a favorite piece of music. These activities are every child's favorite, free entertainment.

Melody

Finally, there is melody. Melody corresponds to our emotions. It gives sound and rhythm its feeling and sensual quality. It is the part of music that can express the hills and valleys of an individual's experience. It goes straight to our heart and feeling center. Melody can uplift our spirit, calm us during times of stress, or move us to tears. Returning to the painting metaphor, melody would be the overall feeling that the painting evokes as we look at it. Does the painting draw us in and create a feeling of peace, excitement, distress, or discomfort? Introducing melody to the earlier sounds and rhythms will help children learn self-expression.

- ☞ Have your children hum a tune or create a melody, adding emotion to sound.

☞ Experiment expressing sounds that are emotional:
happy, sad, funny, and so on.

Melody turns a sound into a personal and unique statement. By playing with sound, rhythm, and melody, our children discover a new vocabulary and a tool to use for expression when words are hard to find.

MATCHING MUSIC TO THE MOOD

As we have seen, different types of music have varying effects on our mind and body. This is important to remember when choosing music for children. If a child needs to be comforted, playing loud drumming music wouldn't be appropriate. It could overstimulate his nervous system and cause further distress. On the other hand, playing a soothing melody by Brahms or Beethoven would slow down his heartbeat and calm and relax his body, achieving the desired effect. So when choosing music, it is important to think of the overall effect and the outcome the music will have on the child.

At nap or bedtime, the right music can be as comforting as a favorite blanket. Select music that is soft and light in texture. Music and rhythm support an infant's sense of well-being. It's best to choose music without words. Words tend to stimulate the brain and nervous system, even in an infant. Listening to words in a song maintains a subtle level of alertness in the mind and body.

When a baby hears soothing instrumental sounds, his brain tends to lose interest and slows to the frequency generated by those sounds. Either slow instrumental music or songs with minimal lyrics are most effective. Lullabies, whale and dolphin sounds, or soft angelic choral music are all sounds that cradle the child in a loving vibration, enhancing relaxation and inviting sleep.

As children get older, expand their musical inventory with stories or guided imagery combined with music. These are helpful if a child is overstimulated and is having trouble focusing. Using this combination after a busy day at school can help a child relax and change gears. If a child is lethargic or pouting, play syncopated Latin music. The fast-paced beat quickly transforms and uplifts her mood. To energize a child or to help motivate her, put on some John Philip Sousa marching music. Children feel much more engaged in their chores or games while listening to music that is stimulating and has a lively beat.

Explore folk songs and nursery rhymes from different cultures. Songs in other languages are a great way to experience the emotional aspect of music. Children hear the song from their feeling center because they cannot understand the words. This teaches them to rely on the rhythm, tone, and overall mood the voice and music create to understand the theme of the song. To locate music of different cultures, look in the "world music" section at music stores or libraries.

The rich variety of rhythm in dance and folk tunes encourages children to experiment with body movement. This enhances their coordination and stimulates motor activity. There are many wonderful rhythmic and up-tempo songs that combine music and learning. For example, there are songs that identify animals and objects, songs that use clapping hands and stomping feet to learn about body parts, and counting songs to learn numbers. Some audiocassettes include activity sheets with games and puzzles. For children learning how to read, *Letter Sounds—Phonics for Beginners* is a good place to start. After learning the basics, there is a follow-up called *Phonics—Vol. I + II.* For help with mathematics, check out *Multiplication Rap* and *Multiplication Rock.*

Walt Disney Records has cassette tapes that include many of their most popular stories. These tapes encourage children to listen to the music to learn the words of their favorite story. Some examples are the *Beauty and the Beast Sing-Along* and *Toy Story Sing-Along.* Each package includes a tape of the story and a booklet to guide the listener and help with the words. All of these tapes make learning fun and hold children's interest longer because of the music.

As children grow, so will their musical interests. The local library is a great source for a variety of music. It also offers information about appropriate music for a child's specific age group. We can use creativity and imagination to choose different styles of music by which our children can express their feelings, relax, stimulate their minds, or allow their creative juices to flow. A variety of selections, rhythms, tones, and melodies allows children to develop their own musical tastes and sparks their natural curiosity to explore the world of music on their own.

EXERCISES TO EXPLORE SOUND, RHYTHM, VOICE, AND MUSIC

Once our children experience the pleasures of sound and rhythm, they will develop an appetite for musical exploration. Nurturing this desire is one of the most wise and loving things we can do as parents. A child who feels free to make sound will also feel safe trying new tasks and venturing into new territory. Ease of self-expression and a healthy body image are the lifelong benefits of early exposure to music-making.

Children introduced to sound and rhythms early in their life develop an easy affinity for musical instruments and often don't need much training. Many of the necessary skills have been cultivated while playing and experimenting with sound, rhythm, and melody.

The first set of exercises that follow begin by exploring the first rhythm that we all experience—the heartbeat.

Reconnecting to Our Heartbeat

The first rhythm and melody we experience in life is the heartbeat experienced within the womb. All newborns are placed on their mother's chests, not to nurse, but to be close to the beat of the mother's heart. The stress and trauma of birth is stabilized by resting on the mother's chest and feeling her heartbeat. The heartbeat from that moment on becomes a powerful anchor and symbol for the child. It represents feelings of warmth, safety, love, caring, nurturing, calm, and balance.

▶ *When we help children reconnect to their own heartbeat and pulse, they again experience those emotions and feelings of safety.*

During times of stress, the heartbeat can also help stabilize and calm them.

Managing stress is a crucial function for our children to learn. When a child feels anxious or worried, their body becomes tense, feelings shut down, and their mind rushes in to take control. They will then react to their world instead of being balanced and responsive within it. Mental clarity can't be achieved without physical calm. Working with the rhythm of the heart gives children a tool to achieve a state of calm during times of stress. Once they understand the power of their own body's rhythm and how to reconnect to it, they can stay grounded and feel safe in their environment. When children feel centered and grounded, they can make responsible choices and decisions.

REFLECTIONS

Close your eyes. Begin breathing gently and deeply.

Listen to the noises around you. What do you hear? Maybe you hear the furnace, the refrigerator, or a buzzing fly.

The "quiet" in our homes is actually made up of all kinds of distinct sounds. Let each one come gently to your attention and then pass, and move on to the next one. When you have run out of audible sounds, just continue to breathe quietly, drawing your attention further inside.

What do you hear now? Your thoughts? Your breathing? Your heartbeat? For just a few moments, place a hand over your heart. Can you feel it beating? If not, find your pulse on your wrist with the thumb of your opposite hand. Take your thumb away and see if you can still feel it.

Let this heartbeat become familiar to you.

The following exercise teaches children how to listen and develop concentration by going inward to find their heartbeat and inner rhythm. When using this exercise with small children, remember to allow for their shorter attention span and adapt accordingly.

Reconnecting Children to Their Heartbeat

Have your children sit with eyes closed and ask them to tell you the sounds they are hearing. Now ask them to just *hear* the sound without saying it out loud. After another minute or so, ask if they can hear any sounds "inside." Give them a little time to listen.

Now have them open their eyes. Show them how to find the pulse in their wrist. Let them know that this is their heartbeat and that this sound will be with them all of their lives. They can come back to this sound whenever they feel nervous, anxious, or scared. Tell them that this can be their internal safety blanket. Give them time to really *feel* its rhythm.

Now ask them to imagine this pulse and heartbeat coming out of the ground. Have them feel Mother Earth's heartbeat and pretend that it is wrapped around them like a warm blanket. Let them know that in times of stress they can always sit on the ground or lean against a tree and feel the heartbeat of Mother Earth. It is always there for them.

Next, ask them to imagine this same pulse beating in members of their family, in different animals, plants, trees, and so on. Be creative and play with this exercise for as long as it is comfortable and fun for the children.

Afterward, ask for feedback. What did the heartbeat sound like? Have the children describe the heartbeat by giving it colors and textures or by singing or dancing the rhythm. How did they feel to discover that every living thing is connected by a heartbeat?

After children are comfortable reconnecting with their heartbeat, they may want to continue exploring their inner landscape. Just as we all need to reconnect to our inner heartbeat and rhythm, it is important for children to know that they each have a unique "inner voice." If they sit quietly and listen, they will hear it.

CONNECTING WITH OUR INNER SOUND/VOICE

It is extremely important for children to find their emerging inner voice. Knowing how to go inside and find a place of peace, or learning how to quiet the mind and clear away the chatter, is invaluable during times of peer pressure and confusion. To help our children focus on their dream, they need to know how to connect to their inner voice.

One way to discover this voice is to sit quietly and slowly focus on our inner ears. Our inner voice may express itself in many different ways. Although we call it a "voice," it may not sound like a voice. It may sound like a wave, or a tone, or a melody running through our head. When doing the following exercise with children, have them take as much time as they need to listen and practice hearing. They may not hear their inner sound the first time they try this exercise.

Finding Our Inner Voice

This exercise uses the sounds of nature as a focus. If possible, do it outdoors. Have the children find a quiet space—leaning against a tree or sitting on a rock. If going outside is not an option, select a time when the house is relatively quiet and put on a tape of recorded nature sounds. There are several series of these tapes such as *Sounds of Nature* or *The Sounds of the Tropical Rain Forest*, which are available in most music stores.

While in a quiet, resting, or contemplative space, have the children listen to the sounds of nature. This time, however, ask that they listen in a different way. Instruct the children to listen to these sounds one by one, until each one has been heard by itself. This gives children a focus for their attention.

When enough time has passed, instruct them to go inward and listen for their inner voice. In the silence, an inner voice may sound like a heartbeat, a waterfall, or a hum. Children may have conversations with themselves. They may feel a pulse or a vibration. Ask them to focus and listen to this sound, their inner song, as long as they like.

During this time, have them connect with any feelings this sound may uncover. Have them listen to any messages that may float to the surface. Let them know that this inner sound is always with them, a constant in their lives they can depend on. Have them practice connecting with it.

Afterward, some children may talk about what they heard. Others may not. Honor their feelings.

This exercise is much more about the process than the result. The experience of being by oneself and listening for what is inside is invaluable for teaching children self-respect and enhancing their confidence. It also teaches concentration and how to clear the mind for decision-making. It is a good way to let feelings surface easily that may not come up otherwise.

By teaching children how to go inward and connect with their inner voice or sound, we are giving them a powerful exercise used by many successful authors, writers, athletes, and top executives. It can be called insight, creativity, contemplation, reflection, refocusing, rebalancing, or going within. The outcome is the same—a clear mind and relaxed body. Many studies have shown that fifteen minutes of this type of meditation is equivalent to a two-hour nap.

LEARNING HOW TO USE OUR VOICE

A parent's voice is a powerful communicator and can have a strong impact and effect on our children. It's usually the first sound our children hear in the morning and the last one they hear at night. Depending on the tone, our voice is music to our children's ears or creates feelings of anxiety and tension. It isn't always *what* we say but *how* we say it that affects those around us.

Our voice is an instrument that conveys different emotions, moods, and feelings. It possesses the power to heal, restore, and regenerate our body, mind, and soul. Did you know that simple humming releases tension and massages our internal organs through its vibration? Or that toning has been used to alleviate pain, relieve symptoms of asthma, and stabilize emotions during panic and anxiety attacks? The benefits our children gain from learning how to use their voice for specific and varying effects are immeasurable. The obvious and most important advantage is that they will be able to communicate clearly and effectively. ▶ *By learning to use their voice, children will gain the confidence and skill to express emotions, give instruction, convey an idea, speak their heart, or voice their dream.*

The first step to clearer communication is to listen to and become comfortable with the sound of our own voices. How

193

many of us cringe when we hear our voice being played back on an answering machine or dislike how we sound speaking in public? This next exercise is a way to become comfortable with how we sound and will give us an avenue to safely explore our speaking voice.

Using Your Voice

Tape-record your voice and listen to it, and then answer these questions: What does your voice sound like? What is the feeling that it conveys? Does your voice originate in your belly or your throat? Do you like the way you sound? If not, play with different tones and rhythms until you do.

Play the tape back to yourself a few times to hear the cadence and rhythm of your speech. To become comfortable with the sound of your own voice, keep listening to it on tape.

After doing the exercise above, let your children try it. Simplify the exercise to match their age.

After exploring the sound of the spoken voice, it is time to add music. The following exercise uses singing as another way to explore and listen to our voices. It develops a number of skills and behaviors at once. It teaches children how to listen and how to reflect what they are hearing. They learn how to discern pitch and rhythm and stimulate speech development through mimicry. And finally, by blending their voice with others, they learn cooperation.

Sing-Along Fun

Have your children hum or sing along with a favorite song. This exercise allows them to hear their voices when others support it.

If a child is shy, sing along in support until she is comfortable singing on her own.

After doing the sing-along exercise, try different variations. Start with a song or nursery rhyme that they are familiar with. After going through it once, have them make up verses and play with rhyming. Let them get silly and make no-nonsense rhymes. The focus is to use the voice for expression and to become comfortable with it.

Expand the exercise by using sounds from nature. Mimic and repeat the sounds. Imitate and repeat the rhythms and melodies.

For infants and very young children, listen to their sounds and imitate them. Mirror their pitch, tone, rhythm, and emotion to communicate with them. Encourage them to repeat the sounds that you make.

Feeling Sound Vibrations

This exercise is a wonderful way to teach children how to relax, clear their mind, and lighten their mood. While they are doing this, encourage them to place a hand where they feel the sound the strongest. To get them going, start at the throat. This is usually the easiest place to feel sound vibrations. Have them use their hands as tools to locate the vibrations on different parts of their body. When they feel a tingling sensation in their hands, they have found a new sound vibration. Have fun and explore the many areas of their body where the sound vibrates.

Have your children look in the mirror and hum a single, sustained note. Watching themselves make the sound strengthens their connection to their voice. Have them play with their voice. Hum high and low, fast and slow. Do they feel tingling?

Have them notice where they feel the sound. This is a vibration created by the sound waves rolling through their bodies.

Now have them hum the sound of *m-m-m* and then *n-n-n*. Does the location of the tingling change? Each vowel or consonant sound vibrates differently. Have them hum each one, noticing where each one resonates in their bodies.

This exercise helps children build their kinesthetic or feeling sense, an important part of body awareness and sensory development. They are also learning to use their voice for self-expression. The next exercise continues with exploring the effects of vibration.

Playing with Vowel Sounds

Have your children practice making long, sustained vowel sounds: *aahh, oh, oo, uu, eee*.

To begin, have your children place a hand on their belly. As they inhale through their nose, expand the air in the belly like a balloon. On the exhale, emit the vowel sound, allowing it to emerge gently and smoothly.

Experiment with higher and lower pitches and go through all the vowel sounds.

Why emphasize vowel sounds? Because they are the most open and easily sustained vocal sounds that we can make. Unlike consonant sounds, sustained vowel sounds massage different body parts and relieve stress. We create powerful vibrations in our body with vowels and will notice a variety of sensations and relaxing aftereffects following this exercise.

▶ *Unlike consonant sounds, sustained vowel sounds massage different body parts and relieve stress.*

Playing with vowels can be used in many different situations. When a child is cranky and irritable, engage her in vowel play to diffuse and shift her energy. During a long car trip, or to ward off boredom, she can pretend that she is an animal, monster, airplane, or spaceship using vowel sounds.

Toning Exercise

Another way to use vowel sounds is toning them. Toning is a natural way to express strong or intense feelings of pleasure or pain. Children release pain by toning. Deeper breathing and toning are particularly effective with asthmatic children as well as for children with high anxiety and stress. A child who has a stomachache could gently sing *"oooo"* or chant *"It huuuuuurrts!"* Toning shifts the child's attention away from the pain, while the vibration that is created can energetically displace and move the pain out of the belly.

- Try toning vowels with your child, singing them over the course of a breath: *"Aaaaaahhh."*
- Try the vowel sounds *oo* and *oh* and *eh* and *ee* as well.
- Try them on low and high notes, softly and loudly.
- Try making your voice into a soft siren, moving it from low to high and back down again.

TOOLS TO AID SELF-EXPRESSION

There are moments of stress and high emotion when children and parents are discordant or out of harmony with each other. When our children don't have an appropriate outlet to express how they're feeling, or if they can't find the right words, blowups and tantrums can occur, making life miserable for all involved. We can use music to coach our children through moments of intense feelings.

This first exercise is excellent for diffusing strong negative emotions by creating a safe space for children to vent and express without getting into trouble. When we see the warning signs of anger and irritation or sibling conflict about to erupt, reach for the drums. Anger has a voice that can be released through drumming, as does happiness, passion, rage, distress, and love. If drums are not available, raid the kitchen for pots and pans and wooden spoons.

Reflecting Moods Exercise #1

1. Pick up a drum, and ask your child to do the same.
2. Ask your child to use the drum to tell you how she feels. As she strikes her drum, answer her by drumming a simple basic beat, such as 1-2-3-4. This supports her and her playing.
3. Reflect the mood she has created on her drum by singing to her, "You sound very angry (happy, earnest, distressed, etc.); is that true?" If you get an affirmative response, ask for more. "Let me hear on the drum just how angry you are." Keep playing a supportive beat as your child lets loose, reflecting her mood.
4. Ask her to keep playing the drum while you listen to her answer. Let her drum until you notice a shift in her energy. Depending on the age of your child and how intensely she is feeling and expressing, the drumming may continue for quite a while. By sustaining a basic

beat beneath your child's expression, you are support-
ively saying that it is all right to express emotions.

To vary this exercise, use other instruments or recorded
music to accompany the child as she bangs on her drum. Just
remember to play in a way that complements her feelings. Even
nonmusicians can pick out sounds on a piano to express rage or
fear. A single note played over and over, escalating in volume,
can easily convey rage or confusion, happiness or excitement.
Singing or humming can also be used as accompaniment. Anyone can make sighing sounds that say, "I am tired," or sing chirpy
birdlike noises that say, "I feel cheerful!"

Be creative. Add recorded music that features accented
rhythm with or without other instruments to the child's drumming. Selections of West African and Native American drumming are ideally suited for this purpose. When the mood shifts,
play some softer, gentler music. Dance and invite your child to
join you; it's a wonderful way to feel the shift in her energy.

This exercise teaches our children appropriate ways to express
intense feelings. It gives them an outlet for those feelings instead
of stuffing or ignoring them. By drumming in support, we demonstrate that feelings are OK, acknowledge them, and give them a
voice. The inner sound and voice are reflected once again. We are
also showing our children that we are there to support them. This
will increase their trust in sharing with us later on.

Reflecting Moods Exercise #2

Try playing a variety of feelings on different instruments. When
you pick up a different instrument, copy the spirit of your child's

playing. Suggest happy, sad, excited, scared, or lonely feelings. The point is to let your child freely explore many different feelings.

Use the same exercises to help her express boundless exuberance and joy. The more experience our children gain in expressing a variety of feelings, the easier it will become to express each of them in healthy ways as they grow up.

Maracas, jingle bells, resonator bells, woodblocks, whistles, small horns, bongo drums, clavas, spoon bells, sticks, castanets, kazoos, and small drums require no musical skill or training to play. Children can just pick them up and let loose, expressing their emotions and feelings quickly and easily.

What if there are no musical instruments in the house? Don't worry. There are always objects that can be used as instruments for the exercises above. Not everyone has a piano or drums, but everybody has pots and pans, jars and glasses, books and tables. Make a game of exploring the sound qualities of different objects. How many instruments can you discover in one room of the house? Pull drawers in or out, tap a wastebasket with a ruler, and crumple a paper bag.

Simple instruments can also be made cheaply and easily. Here are a few basic ideas:

- A small, sturdy container partially filled with beans, rice, or pebbles makes a rattle.
- The bottom of a cooking pot or empty oatmeal container makes a drum. Tap on it with hands, spoons, or chopsticks.
- Place rubber bands of differing sizes and thickness over a small open box and pluck away on your box banjo.

☞ Fill jars or glasses with different amounts of water and tap them with a spoon. Can you match them with the notes of a scale?

We can also teach our children to think of their bodies as instruments. We all use our voice to make music but forget to incorporate the rest of our bodies. We can make many sounds and noises with it.

To help motivate children and to give them an example, play some Bobby McFerrin music. He is a vocalist who uses his voice and body to create rhythms, melodies, and sounds and turns them into songs. The exercise below will help to start the exploration. How many types of sounds can you and your child discover?

Our Body as an Instrument

Begin this activity by having your child clap his hands, snap his fingers, and then rub his hands or fingernails together.

Next, have him open his mouth like he is saying *ooo*. Then have him lightly tap his fingers on his cheeks. By slightly changing his mouth shape, different pitches can be created. Play "Row, Row, Row Your Boat" or any favorite song this way.

Now your child can play his nose! Have him hold his left nostril shut with the index finger of his left hand and tap the right nostril with his right hand as he hums a tune. Play "Guess This Tune" together.

How many different ways can your child make music using his feet? Have him tap a song with his feet or sprinkle sand on the floor and make shuffling sounds.

MUSICAL SELF-EXPRESSION FOR THE ENTIRE FAMILY

So far in this chapter, we've explored many ways that sound, rhythm, and music can be used for self-expression, stress resolution, and one-on-one communication with a child. What about using music with the whole family to relieve tensions, open up new channels of communication, and help move energy? Family members can use Musical Round Robin to safely express feelings that may have remained uncovered and also have some plain old fun.

Musical Round Robin

In a Musical Round Robin, use either voices or instruments (or both). In any Round Robin, the main point is to create a setting where every participant is equal. To begin, have the family gather in a room and bring along any instruments that are available. Remember that household objects or voices can also be instruments. The makeup of the family band isn't important. Using voices, kazoos, whistles, salad bowls, and glasses is just as effective as using drums, pianos, and guitars. Let everyone gravitate toward the instrument of their choice.

Explain the ground rules before starting:

- Playing together means listening to each other and respecting everyone's feelings.
- Each instrument has a voice of its own, just like we do, and each voice is equal in importance. The youngest member who can only ring a bell is just as important as an older child who plays the piano or guitar.
- For each round there is a leader or conductor. Every member of the family will take a turn being the con-

ductor. This gives everyone the experiences of leading and of following. Decide the order of the conductors to avoid confusion during the rounds. The conductor sets the dynamics and rules. He or she is responsible for the flow of the round, deciding when to start, which family member goes first, who goes next, and how long each person plays.

Before the Round Robin begins, encourage the children to practice for a few minutes on their instrument or with their voice to warm up. Ask them to take a moment to think about a feeling they may want to express through their music.

Round One: The conductor signals the first participant to begin. Perhaps the piano starts, followed by a guitar, and then the maracas. While the first person plays, everyone else listens. Then the conductor stops the first person and signals for the next one to play.

When everyone has had a turn playing, round one is over. Take time to ask for feedback. What instrument worked best? What didn't work and why? What feelings were heard as each person played? Did everyone feel listened to? Did everyone listen?

Round Two: In round two, everyone plays together. The conductor cues the first person to play. Then one by one, he cues everyone else to join in. For instance, the conductor may start with a rhythm instrument to establish a basic beat. Then each person contributes to the homemade orchestra.

When it is time to end the jam session, the conductor taps each member's shoulder one by one to stop. Again, take time for feedback.

These are just the basics of Musical Round Robin to get the family started. There can be as many variations as there are conductors. One conductor may request family members to play according to age order, starting with the youngest. Another may want the parents to perform throughout the round, adding and subtracting various siblings. Everyone will feel more comfortable after a few rounds. It takes time to get accustomed to making music in a group and concentrating on all the different dynamics.

Musical Improvisation

Another way to incorporate musical expression with the entire family is through improvisation. Improvisation is expressing musical ideas spontaneously. It is a way to have free-flowing musical conversation without a specific structure. Gather the family together and bring along instruments, noisemakers, and so on. Each member can either choose an instrument or use their voice. Improvising is wonderful because it can't be done wrong! It is expression based on fun and exploration. Playing along while someone is improvising is like learning a new language. We hear a musical phrase from their voice or instrument and try to repeat it, copying the quality and emotion. This requires listening and feeling the music and emotions being expressed. As in Musical Round Robin, ask for feedback when one round is completed.

One parent can start off on "voice" by singing "ba-boob-a-da ba ba bah, ba-boob-a-da dee." Then one child joins in with a rattle playing whatever rhythm the parent is singing. The next child supports the lead voice and the rattle by doing a "boom-chick, boom-chick, boom-chick" beat with the spoons.

Now another joins in by playing bells on the off-beats, the ones that aren't accented by the rattle. In no time you are jamming! Gradually the parent fades in volume so that someone else can have the lead, introducing a new beat and musical idea that everyone else will support.

Family members can switch instruments during the improvisation. Allow everyone a chance to "lead the pack." This is a good way to build confidence and self-esteem. During feedback time, ask each child how it felt to be out front leading the group. What did they like or not like about it?

Musical exploration may be relatively new to some families. If no one knows how to begin, ask a family member to start whistling how their day went or to express how they are feeling on the kazoo. Imitate different moods through music. How does happy, sad, angry, or joyful sound? Then have everyone join in to help break the ice. After expressing emotions through music, experiment with natural sounds. See if the family can create the sounds of a thunderstorm, waves crashing against rocks, or a chorus of animals howling under a full moon. It should be enlightening to hear how each child expresses his feelings or creates music from his imagination.

Another way to improvise is to create original songs. Speak or sing feelings to recorded music while others hum or play an instrument in support. Use drums for "loud" feelings and gentle sounds for quieter, more introspective moods. Some of the themes below can be used for improvisation:

☞ I have a dream.
☞ My dream wants to say. . .

- I'm so tired.
- I'm full of energy.
- You look happy/sad/angry tonight.
- The "please" song.
- The "no" song.
- The "yes" song.
- Love is a name called . . .
- I love it when you do . . .
- I'd like attention.
- Leave me alone! Stop picking on me.
- I need a hug.
- The ten things I love about you are . . .

Musical improvisation isn't just for special gatherings. It works well one-on-one and during moments of conflict throughout the day. When children start to tease each other or someone comes home from school with hurt feelings, sing their mood or sentiments back to them. Echo and reflect their feelings. Or sing a supportive line like, "You sound very sad." Encourage them to join in. Continue until there is a shift in the intensity or quality of the child's feelings.

Through song, expressing moods and reactions becomes a game instead of an interrogation. Children tend to open up more quickly and feel safer sharing when it's fun.

Use musical improvisation while shuttling the children to soccer practice, grocery shopping, or on trips. It's a great tool to use when stuck in a traffic jam. One common way we express our feelings during these moments is to fume and mutter sounds under our breath. Then our children usually start to move around and fidget, annoying each other and us because they don't have a proper outlet for their energy.

To shift everyone's mood, we can start to make sounds that convey frustration. Invite everyone to join in to release the tension that comes from being bottled up together in the car. Then slowly bring the noise level down in volume and move on to creating a song, such as, "Do I really need to worry when I'm in a hurry?" Ask them to join in by asking, "What rhymes with *hurry?*" They might answer, "Furry!" Have them sing a line that ends in the word *furry*. If they get too loud or rambunctious, ask them to sing their line in a whisper. Make a game out of who can whisper their answer the quietest and still be heard.

A SPRINGBOARD TO GREATER EXPRESSION

There are many different and varying ways to explore the power of music with children. Take these exercises and use them as a springboard. Encourage children to improvise or to add their own flavor to an exercise. Again, the whole idea is to foster expression through music and to teach the building blocks for the dream—esteem, empowerment, and wholeness.

Musical expression is a wonderful tool to keep handy. At the first sign of sibling rivalry, remember to use a "Reflecting Moods" exercise. If a child is anxious about studying for a test, play some baroque music to calm and relax his body and create a state of mental receptivity. Music can enhance every aspect of our children's lives. It is up to us to show them how and to invite them to explore this wonderful medium.

Epilogue

Your children will see what you're all about by what you live
rather than what you say.

Wayne Dyer

Our task as parents is before us: Will we open doors and show our children
how to walk through—to nurture their gifts, dream, positively succeed, and
be happy?

Remember those times as a parent when you felt the most inspired, successful, and really happy? We want to memorize those genuine moments of heart. The inspired feelings uplift us and remind us that we bring joy to our lives and our children's lives. We don't wait for joy to happen; rather, we choose inspiration at each moment we parent. In these heartfelt depths of inspiration, we are the most sincere, honest, and authentic in our parenting and show real congruence to our children. Inspired parenting is congruence, consistency, choice-making, awareness, and caring.

CONGRUENCE AND CONSISTENCY

In the introduction, I addressed the freedom that we feel when we dissolve all of our "shoulds" and "oughts" about parenting. Then, there are no more small voices in our heads judging, condemning, cajoling, denying, or guilt-tripping. Rather, we become emotionally, intuitively, and instinctually connected to and aware of our children. We can see more clearly their thoughts, feelings, games, fears, gifts, talents, and dreams. We are more confident in ourselves as parents, and we convey that energy to our children.

Congruence is being in tune with ourselves about how we feel and how we respond in any given moment. If we are congruent, we are using our mind to look at things rationally, *and* we are using our feelings to determine if there is anything deeper, at the nonverbal level or gut level, that calls to our attention.

An example of incongruence is if you were to hit a child out of anger while something inside your heart is screaming, "Don't!" Another would be when you want to be right about an issue between you and your child. You just want the child to hear you, accept it, and get over it. But your child questions you, knows that you are pushing your power around for your convenience. Would you rather be right or would you rather be happy? To be congruent in this situation would be to drop your agenda of needing to be right. The actions that you subsequently choose would be for the higher good of you and your child. This may be the same outcome of your agenda, and you can accomplish it with more transparency and consideration for all involved.

Congruence is being attuned to your feelings as well as your thoughts. It is making choices for the higher good of you and your family. It is being as emotionally honest as you can be in the moment and making effective choices within your parameters. It is not apologizing or complaining about the choices you make but selecting actions and understanding the consequences.

When Julian's thirteen-year-old stepson came to live with her and her new husband of nine months, Julian thought that the honeymoon period was over. Trying to be a good stepparent, she asked her stepson and husband to sit down one morning to set up some household agreements. She and her husband had prepared some suggestions to share with the stepson. The stepson had done the same. They asked their stepson to agree to room cleanliness, hygiene parameters, food preparation, laundry schedules, and the usual family routines. He simply said, "No." When he lived with his biological mother, he'd fixed his own food, done his own laundry, rarely cleaned his room, and set his own schedule, and he had no intention of changing his life. Julian saw that her stepson had never lived with a family and had been taught to be independent. Should she insist that he change now? For her sake or the sake of "family"?

After much discussion, they each dropped their personal plans and agreed to see what would work for kitchen, laundry, and room-cleaning schedules. This decision felt congruent to the three family members because it was honest and not complicated with hidden agendas. They demonstrated mutual respect through their discussions. Julian gave up the idea of exerting influence on her stepson, realizing that he had been living as an adult for several years. Her husband had always been a friend to his son, and this relationship grew. Having participated in establishing the guidelines, the stepson felt freer to communicate and join in family activities.

CHOICE-MAKING

Free of agendas then, the parenting choices that we make in any given moment usually come from a combination of our emotions and our intuition, not necessarily our logic. In that instant of choice, we are left with the present moment, the heart of the matter, the context of the situation, and the question, "What works here?"

This is our time to take a deeper breath and watch for certain feelings and behaviors: *What is the undercurrent? What am I feeling? How can I communicate? What do I need to do?*

All of these split-second thoughts and observations usually happen so quickly that we have to retrain ourselves to not habitually react but rather to pause a moment and choose an effective response. *Nurture Your Child's Gift* has given you reflections for inner growth to help you see situations more clearly. Moments of pause allow you to breathe deeply, shift your energy, check in with your intuition, think through an answer, and reframe negativity into a more affirming approach.

Perhaps the real power of inspired parenting is in the moment of pause when you can "check in" and be sure of yourself—the ultimate confidence builder that says you are doing what you know to do in any given instant. You are aware in each moment, and you make your choice for parenting. Make yours a positive one!

In the introduction, I invited all parents to see our children as living souls who have a unique gift and a dream to fulfill. This requires a transformation in our thinking and a revolution in the way we treat our children. The motto of this transformation revolution is very simple: *Be aware and care!*

AWARENESS AND CARING

While having breakfast with friends one Saturday morning, I

noticed a thirty-ish father, a large muscular man, having a meal with his son, who appeared to be about three years of age.

While waiting for food, the boy became restless and slid around on his side of the booth. Then he slid right down and sat on the floor under the table. The action embarrassed his father, who repeatedly said, "Get up. Don't do that. Get up now."

When his son didn't respond, the father tried kicking the boy out from under the table. The father's foot was large and struck his son squarely at the base of the spine, although the father could not see this above the table. The boy's response was to freeze, not move, and continue sitting under the table. I observed that the boy froze in response to where his father kicked him, not out of defiance but out of pain. When you strike a blow to the spine, the ripples of pain cause one to react with fear, not motivation to please. The boy couldn't move because he was hurt.

Apply the motto, *Be aware and care*, to such situations. The father was not aware of where his foot hit or how he was physically hurting his son. The father did not care for the boy's agitation or comfort—just his own embarrassment. Being aware would mean speaking to the child differently, inviting the child to sit on his lap or back on the seat, or trying another activity. Caring for the child might mean not kicking. Instead, the father could check to see why the boy didn't respond, not assume that the boy was deliberately defying him.

Wholeness

When we approach parenting from a viewpoint of holism, we are committing to helping our children's gifts unfold throughout their lives. We understand from mindbody research that children have specific temperaments that are genetically determined to some extent. However, the acculturation and education we provide through our parenting shapes that temperament according to our values and social expectations. Parents *do* make a difference!

Attuned to our children's patterns and expressions as they move through each developmental phase, we can help them manage their emotions so that they mature as socially responsible adults. Acceptance of our children's temperaments and emotional patterns enables them to learn from their mistakes and establishes a baseline of inner confidence to face the challenges and changes of daily life. We can help them learn from their mistakes and gain self-trust to keep going, solve problems, and look for new solutions.

The techniques provided in *Nurture Your Child's Gift* inspire us to consistently develop new ways to deal with everyday life and prevent us from falling into habitual—and often unsatisfying— parenting patterns. Breathing, music, imagery, stories, affirmations, problem-solving, and empowerment approaches help keep us and our children focused on those crucial choices we make each moment. All of these approaches are easy and natural. It is your commitment to parenting excellence that will make a difference in your child's life.

This parenting revolution helps restore visions and dreams for our children as well as for us as parents. We all have hope, and we all need something to look forward to. This dream holds a child's life intact and gently nudges one toward its aspirations. This vision is a suble thread so fine that we rarely glimpse it. This is why we try to be aware, to care, and to be present in each moment of our choices.

You are invited to join our parenting revolution! It starts within each of us as we make positive and inspired parenting choices for the good of our child and family.

Visit *www.inspiredparenting.org*. Post your stories, caring messages, and encouragement to other parents on the message board, and we'll spread the word that we parents care enough to be aware and to make our choices from a place of love.

This is the way that change happens—one person at a time, sharing with another person, until you can see the change in your world.

Notes

Introduction

1. Department of Health and Human Services, National Institutes of Health, Office for Alternative Medicine, *Report on Alternative Medicine* (Washington, D.C.: U.S. Government Printing Office).

Chapter 1

1. Mary Crowley, "Do Kids Need Prozac?" *Newsweek*, October 20, 1997, 73–74.

2. James Hillman, *The Soul's Code: In Search of Character and Calling* (New York: Random House, 1996), 13.

Chapter 2

1. M. Neely-Martinez, "The Smarts That Count," *HR Magazine*, November 1997, 71–78.

2. Daniel Goleman, *Emotional Intelligence: Why It Can Matter More than IQ for Character, Health and Lifelong Achievement* (New York: Bantam, 1995), 44.

3. Stephen Hein, *EQ for Everybody* (Clearwater, Florida: Aristotle Press, 1999), 58–59.

4. Goleman, *Emotional Intelligence*, 207

5. J. Achterberg and G. Frank Lawlis, *Bridges of the Bodymind: Behavioral Approaches to Health Care* (Champaign, Ill.: Institute for Personality and Ability Testing, 1980), 239.

6. T. Berry Brazelton, *Heart Start: The Emotional Foundations of School Readiness* (Arlington, Va.: National Center for Clinical Infant Programs, 1992), preface, quoted in Goleman, *Emotional Intelligence*, 193.

7. Goleman, *Emotional Intelligence*, 90.

8. David G. Myers, *The Pursuit of Happiness: Discovering the Pathway to Fulfillment, Well-Being, and Enduring Personal Joy* (New York: Avon Books, 1993), 207.

9. Rick Snyder, "Where There's Hope, There's Life," *Berkeley Wellness Letter*, March 1992, 2–3.

10. S. Keleman, *Emotional Anatomy* (Berkeley, Calif.: Center Press, 1985), 90.

11. Joel Robertson, *Peak-Performance Living* (San Francisco: HarperSanFrancisco, 1997), 4.

Chapter 3

1. James Cameron, "Understanding Your Child's Temperament," *Mind/Body Health Newsletter* 6, no. 2 (1997), 3.

2. J. Kagan, "Sanguine and Melancholic Temperaments in Children," *The Harvard Mental Health Newsletter* 13, no. 4 (1996), 4–6.

3. Ibid.

4. Ibid.

5. Reprinted with permission from James Cameron, "Understanding Your Child's Temperament," *Mind/Body Health Newsletter* 6, no. 2 (1997), 5.

6. Reprinted with permission from James Cameron, "Understanding Your Child's Temperament," 4–5.

7. Howard Gardner, *Frames of Mind: The Theory of Multiple Intelligences* (New York: Basic Books, HarperCollins, 1983), 3–5.

8. Charles Johnston, *Necessary Wisdom: Meeting the Challenge of a New Cultural Maturity* (Berkeley, Calif.: Celestial Arts, 1991), 106–112.

9. Ibid, 111.

Chapter 7

1. Raymond Starr Jr., quoted in Marian Diamond and Janet Hopson, *Magic Trees of the Mind: How to Nurture Your Child's Intelligence, Creativity, and Healthy Emotions from Birth through Adolescence* (New York: Dutton, 1998), 131.

Chapter 8

1. Daniel Goleman, *Emotional Intelligence: Why It Can Matter More Than IQ for Character, Health and Lifelong Achievement* (New York: Bantam, 1995), 166.

2. Candace Pert, H. E. Dreher, and M. R. Ruff, "The Psychosomatic Network: Foundations for Mind-Body Medicine," *Journal of Alternative Therapies in Health and Medicine* 4, no. 4 (July 1998), 30.

3. Ibid.

4. Rachel Naomi Remen, "Feeling Well: A Clinician's Casebook," *Advances* 6, no. 2, 43–49.

5. Eugene Arnold, *Childhood Stressors* (New York: John Wiley & Sons, 1990), 2.

Chapter 9

1. Herbert Benson, *The Relaxation Response* (New York: William Morrow, 1975).

Chapter 10

1. J. W. Shields, "Lymph, lymph glands, and homeostasis," *Lymphology* 25, no. 4 (1992), 147–153.
2. Richard Miller, "The Psychophysiology of Respiration: Eastern and Western Perspectives," *Yoga Journal*, May/June 1994.
3. Gunnel Minett, *Breath and Spirit: Rebirthing as a Healing Technique* (San Francisco: The Aquarian Press, 1994), 95.
4. Sheldon Saul Hendler, *The Oxygen Breakthrough: Thirty Days to an Illness Free Life* (New York: William Morrow, 1989), 96.
5. Tom Goode, *Cosmic Waltz*, compact disk and audiocassette (Boulder, Colo.: International Breath Institute, 1999).

Chapter 11

1. Colin Rose, *Accelerated Learning* (New York: Dell, 1985), 93.
2. J. E. Landreth and H. F. Landreth, "Effects of Music on Physiological Response," *Journal of Research in Music Education* 22 (1974), 4–12.
3. Don Campbell, *The Mozart Effect* (New York: Avon Books, 1997), 14.
4. Howard Gardner, *Frames of Mind: The Theory of Multiple Intelligences* (New York: Basic Books, Harper Collins, 1983), 105.

Resources

PARENTING BOOKS AND AUDIOCASSETTES

A Good Enough Parent: A Book on Child Rearing. Bruno Bettelheim and Anne Freedgood. Vintage Books, 2000 (ISBN: 0394757769).

Awakened Heart Parenting:Relating to and Raising Children (Infants and Toddlers) as Spirit Beings. Helen Hood. Dancing Heart Press, 1997 (ISBN: 0965553205).

Bringing Out the Winner in Your Child. John Croyle with Ken Abraham. Cumberland House, 1998 (ISBN: 1888952903).

Children Learn What They Live: Parenting to Inspire Values. Dorothy Law Nolte, Rachel Harris, and Jack Canfield. Workman Publishing, 1998 (ISBN: 0761109196).

Creative Journal for Parents: A Guide to Unlocking Your Natural Parenting Wisdom. Lucia Capacchione. Shambhala Publications, 2000 (ISBN: 1570623996).

Easy to Love, Difficult to Discipline: Seven Basic Skills for Turning Conflict into Cooperation. Becky A. Bailey, Ph.D. William Morrow, 2000 (ISBN: 0688161162).

Emotional Development and Emotional Implications. Peter Salovey and David J. Sluyter, editors. Basic Books, 1997 (ISBN: 0465095879).

Emotionally Intelligent Parenting: How to Raise a Self-Disciplined, Responsible, Socially Skilled Child. Maurice J. Elias, Ph.D., Steven E. Tobias, and Brian S. Friedlander, Ph.D. Fireside, 1998 (ISBN: 0201073978).

Emotional Literacy: To Be a Different Kind of Smart. Rob Bocchino. Corwin Press, 1999 (ISBN: 0803968248).

How to Behave So Your Children Will To. Sal Severe, Ph.D. Viking Press, 2000 (ISBN: 0670891533); audiocassette: Simon & Schuster, 2000 (ISBN: 0743500571).

How to Raise a Child with a High EQ: A Parent's Guide to Emotional Intelligence. Lawrence E. Shapiro. HarperCollins, 1998 (ISBN: 0060928913).

How to Raise Your Child's Emotional Intelligence: 101 Ways to Bring Out the Best in Your Children and Yourself. Allen Nagy, Ph.D., and Geraldine Nagy, Ph.D. Heartfelt Publications, 1999 (ISBN: 0966428706).

How to Really Love Your Child. Ross Campbell, M.D. Chariot Victor Books, 1992 (ISBN: 0896930661).

Moms Come First! Three Steps to Enlightened Parenting (The Heart, Soul, and Joy of Parenting for the New Millennium). Dvorah Adler. Sunstar Publishing, 2000 (ISBN: 1887472630).

Personality Plus for Parents: Understanding What Makes Your Child Tick.
Florence Littaver. Fleming H. Revell, 2000 (ISBN: 0800757378).

Positive Child Guidance. Darla Ferris Miller. Delmar Publishers,
1999 (ISBN: 0766803600).

Raising Compassionate, Courageous Children in a Violent World. Dr.
Janice Cohn. Longstreet Press, 1996 (ISBN: 1563522764).

*Raising Spiritual Children in a Material World: Introducing Spirituality
into Family Life.* Phil Catalfo. Berkley Publishing, 1997 (ISBN:
0425149544).

*Raising Your Spirited Child: A Guide for Parents Whose Child Is More
Intense, Sensitive, Perceptive, Persistent, Energetic.* Mary Sheedy
Kurcinka. HarperPerennial Library, 1992 (ISBN: 0060923288);
audiocassette: Harper Audio, 1999 (ISBN: 0694522015).

Raising Your Spirited Child Workbook. Mary Sheedy Kurcinka.
HarperCollins, 1998 (ISBN: 0060952407).

*Spiritual Parenting: A Guide to Understanding and Nurturing the Heart of
Your Child.* Hugh and Gayle Prather. Crown Publishing, 1997
(ISBN: 0517888319); audiocassette: Audio Literature, 1996
(ISBN: 0517888319).

*Strangers in the Nest: Do Parents Really Share Their Child's Intelligence,
Personality and Character?* David B. Cohen, Ph.D. John Wiley &
Sons, 1999 (ISBN: 0471319228).

Teaching Your Children Joy. Linda and Richard Eyre. Fireside, 1994
(ISBN: 0671887254); audiocassette: *Teaching Your Children Values.*

Linda and Richard Eyre. Simon & Schuster, 1993 (ISBN: 0671044877).

Ten Principles for Spiritual Parenting: Nurturing Your Child's Soul. Mimi Doe Walch. HarperPerennial Library, 1998 (ISBN: 0060952415).

The Heart of Parenting: Raising an Emotionally Intelligent Child (audiocassette). John Mordechai Gottman and Joan DeClaire. Audio Renaissance, 1997 (ISBN: 0684838656).

The Hurried Child: Growing Up Too Fast Too Soon. David Elkind. Perseus Press, 1989 (ISBN: 0201073978).

The Mozart Effect for Children: Awakening Your Child's Mind, Health, and Creativity with Music. Don Campbell. William Morrow, 2000 (ISBN: 0896930661).

The Path of Parenting: Twelve Principles to Guide Your Journey. Vimala McClure. New World Library, 1999 (ISBN: 1577310780).

The Positive Minute. Will Horton. W. Whorton, 2000 (ISBN: 1892274027).

The Seven Habits of Highly Effective Families: Building a Beautiful Family Culture in a Turbulent World. Stephen R. Covey and Sandra Merrill Covey. Golden Book Publishing, 1998 (ISBN: 0307440850); audiocassette: Covey Leadership Center, 1997 (ISBN: 1883219965).

The Seven Spiritual Laws for Parents. Deepak Chopra. Crown Publishers, 1997 (ISBN: 060960077X); audiocassette: Random House, 1997 (ISBN: 0679460411).

The Wise Child: A Spiritual Guide to Nurturing Your Child's Intuition. Sonia Choquette, Ph.D. Three Rivers Press, 1999 (ISBN: 0609803999).

Transforming the Difficult Child: The Nurtured Heart Approach. Howard Glasser and Jennifer Easley. Center for the Difficult Child, 1999 (ISBN: 0967050707).

Understanding Your Child's Temperament. William B. Carey, M.D. IDG Books Worldwide, 1999 (ISBN: 0028628268).

Whole Child/Whole Parent. Polly Berrien Berends. HarperCollins, 1997 (ISBN: 0060928182).

MUSIC FOR PARENTS AND CHILDREN

Awaken (healing) (audio CD). Dorothea Joyce Productions, 2000 ([248] 761-9428; 1-888-re-joyce; DorotheaJoyce@aol.com).

Baby's Song (audio CD). Dorothea Joyce Productions, 2000 ([248] 761-9428; 1-888-re-joyce; DorotheaJoyce@aol.com).

Blanket Full of Dreams (audio CD). Cathy Fink and Marcy Marxer. Rounder Records, 1996 (ASIN: B0000003GR).

Circus Magic (audio CD). Linda Arnold. Youngheart Music, 2000 (1-800-444-4287; http://www.younghrt.com).

Cosmic Waltz (relaxing music and breathing program) (audiocassettes). Tom Goode, N.D. International Breath Institute, 1999 (http://www.transformbreathing.com or www.inspiredparenting.org).

Goodnight Blue (audio CD). Kid Rhino, 2000 (1-800-432-0020; www.kidrhino.com).

Googol On! (audio CD). Scott Johnson. Googol Press, 1998 (ASIN: B00000DA1O).

Lullabies for Little Visionaries (audio CD). Danae Shanti and the Inspired Child Choir. Sounding Free Productions, 2000 ([303] 530-3920; http://www.soundingfree.net).

Monkey in the Middle (audio CD). Daddy a Go Go. Boyd's Tone, 2000 (ASIN: B00004NS07).

The Mozart Effect—Music for Babies—Playtime to Sleepytime (audio CD). Leopold Mozart. Wea/Atlantic/Children's Group, 1998 (ASIN: B00000DA1O).

Mozart Effect—Music for Children. Vol. 1: Tune Up Your Mind (audio CD). Don Campbell. Children's Group, 1997 (UPC: 68478429129; http://www.mozarteffect.com).

Mozart Effect—Music for Children. Vol. 2: Relax, Daydream and Draw (audio CD). Don Campbell. Children's Group, 1997 (UPC: 68478429228).

Mozart Effect—Music for Children. Vol. 3: Mozart in Motion (audio CD). Don Campbell. Children's Group, 1997 (UPC: 68478429327).

Mozart Effect: Nighty Night (audio CD). Don Campbell. Children's Group, 2000 (UPC: 68478433225).

Music for the Mozart Effect. Vol. 1: Strengthen the Mind (audio CD). Spring Hill Records, 1998 (UPC: 718795650149).

Music for the Mozart Effect. Vol. 2: Heal the Body (audio CD). Don Campbell. Spring Hill Records, 1998 (UPC: 718795650224).

Night Songs and Lullabies (audio CD). Compass Records, 2000 ([615] 320-7672; http://www.compassrecords.com).

Oquixpi: Creative Music for Children (audiocassette). Maruja Lenero, 1999 (ASIN: B00004U1R9; http://www.oquixpi.com).

Pillow Full of Wishes (audio CD). Cathy Fink and Marcy Marxer. Rounder Select, 2000 (ASIN: B00003W89Z).

Singin' in the Bathtub (audio CD). John Lithgow. Sony/Wonder, 1999 (ASIN: B0000018A3).

Songs for Parents and Kids Too! (audio CD). 1999 (ASIN: B00003WGOK).

Toddler's Sing: Music for Little People (audio CD). Toddler's Sing. Wea/Atlantic/Rhino, 1998 (ASIN: B00000C41T).

We Can All Be Free: A Seminar in Concert for Inner Peace (audio CD). Dorothea Joyce Productions, 2000 ([248] 761-9428; 1-888-re-joyce; DorotheaJoyce@aol.com).

World Playground (audio CD). Various artists. Putumayo, 1999 (ASIN: B00000JT4P).

CATALOGS FOR PARENTS AND CHILDREN

Chinaberry, 2780 Via Orange Way, Suite B, Spring Valley, CA 91978; http://www.chinaberry.com.

HearthSong, 170 Professional Center Drive, Rohnert Park, CA 94928; http://www.hearthsong.com.

Music for Little People, P.O. Box 1460, Redway, CA 95560-1460; http://www.musicforlittlepeople.com.

HELPFUL WEB SITES FOR PARENTS

ABC's of Parenting (http://www.abcparenting.com)

A Listening Ear (http://pil.net/~msteach)

American Coalition for Fathers and Children
   (http://www.acfc.org)

Awesome Library (http://www.awesomelibrary.org/parent.html)

Breastfeeding and Parenting Resources on the Internet
   (http://www.prairienet.org/laleche/other.html)

Canadian Parents Online (http://www.canadianparents.com)

Child.net (http://www.child.net)

Colorado Parent and Information Resource Center
   (http://www.cpirc.org/links.htm)

Crafts for Kids and Parenting Advice
   (http://www.childfun.com)

CTW Family Workshop (http://www.ctw.org)

Cyber Patrol (http://www.cyberpatrol.com)

Daddys Home (http://www.daddyshome.com)

Daily Tips4Parents (http://www.tips4parents.com)

Dear Parents (http://www.dearparents.com)

Dr. Paula (http://www.drpaula.com)

Entertainment Reviews for Parents (http://www.screenit.com)

Entrepreneurial Parent (http://en-parent.com)

eScore (http://www.escore.com)

Family.com (http://family.go.com)

FamilyEducation Network (http://www.familyeducation.com)

Family Fun Magazine (http://www.familyfun.com)

Family Internet (http://www.familyinternet.com)

Family Magazine (http://www.thefamilycorner.com)

Family Nation (http://www.familynation.net)

Fathering Magazine (http://www.fathersworld.com)

Father's World (http://www.fathersworld.com)

Give Six Seconds for Emotional Intelligence
     (http://www.6seconds.org/index.shtml)

Health Answers (http://www.healthanswers.com)

Healthy Child (http://www.healthychild.com)

HealthyKids.com (http://www.healthykids.com)

Home Income Producing Parents (http://www.hipparents.org)

HomeworkCentral.com (http://www.homeworkcentral.com)

InspiredParenting.org (http://inspiredparenting.org)

KidsDoctor (http://www.kidsdoctor.com)

KidSource (http://www.kidsource.com)

MoM (http://www.avsweb.com/mom)

Moms Online (http://www.momsonline.com)

Mothering (http://www.mothering.com)

Myria: Relationships and Parenting
     (http://myria.com/relationships)

My Shoes (multicultural perspective) (http://myshoes.com)

National Center for Fathering (http://www.fathers.com)

National Child Care Information Center (http://nccic.org)

National Parent Information Network (http://www.npin.org)

National Parenting Center (http://www.tnpc.com)

Net Nanny (http://www.netnanny.com)

Not Just for Kids! (http://www.night.net/kids)

OnePlace (http://www2.oneplace.com)

ParenthoodWeb (http://www.parenthoodweb.com)

Parenting Online (http://www.parenting.com/parenting)

Parenting Q&A (http://www.parenting-qa.com)

Parenting Special Needs (http://specialchildren.about.com/
    parenting/specialchildren)

ParentNews (http://parent.net)

Parents Helping Parents (http://www.php.com)

Parent Soup (http://www.parentsoup.com)

ParentsPlace.com (http://www.parentsplace.com)

Parents Place Chat
    (http://www.parentsplace.com/messageboards)

ParentsTalk (http://www.parents-talk.com)

Parent's Television Council (http://www.parentsvorg)

Parents Without Partners
    (http://www.parentswithoutpartners.org)

PEP: Parents, Educators, and Publishers
    (http://www.microweb.com/pepsite)

Positive Parenting (http://www.positiveparenting.com)

Single Dad's Index
    (http://www.vix.com/pub/men/single-dad.html)

Site for Parents
    (http://www.ala.org/parentspage/greatsites/parent.html)

Spilt Milk (http://www.spiltmilk.net)

Spiritual Parenting (http://www.spiritualparenting.com)

Sports Parent (http://www.sportsparent.com)

Stay at Home Parents
(http://www.homeparents.miningco.com)

Stepfamily Foundation (http://www.stepfamily.org)

SuperKids Educational Software Review
(http://www.superkids.com)

The Family Room (http://www.thelaboroflove.com/forum)

The Idea Box (http://www.theideabox.com)

The Informed Parent (http://www.informedparent.com)

The Natural Family Site (http://www.bygpub.com/natural)

The School Report (http://www.theschoolreport.com)

The Whole Family Center
(http://www.wholefamily.com/indexIE.html)

Timely Tips for Families
(http://www.msue.msu.edu/msue/cyf/cyftips.html)

Tips for Working Mothers (http://fleury.coastalw.com)

Today's Parent (http://www.todaysparent.com)

20ish Parents (http://www.20ishparents.com)

Twins Magazine (http://www.twinsmagazine.com)

UC Berkeley Parents Network (http://parents.berkeley.edu)

Wise Women of the Web
(http://www.neosoft.com/~acoustic/www.html)

Women-networking.com (http://www.women-networking.com)

Women's Work (http://www.wwork.com)

Work at Home Moms (http://www.wahm.com)

Personal and Professional Training Programs

International Breath Institute
2525 Arapahoe Avenue, Bldg. E-4, PMB 287
Boulder, CO 80302; www.transformbreathing.com
Telephone: (303) 444-8615; fax: (303) 444-5095
   Offers information, training seminars, and professional certification in the TransformBreathing™ Energy Management System and the Full Wave Breath™ for persons of all ages and health conditions.

Pathways to Success and Self-Reliance/Transformational Journeys
Donna Packard, M.Ed., CTBF
P.O. Box 318, York Harbor, ME 03911; (207) 363-1925
   Offers individual and group programs utilizing breath, imagery, and sound to promote wellness of mind, body, and spirit. Motivational programs that empower participants to own their dreams, build a sense of self-worth, and break through barriers that may keep them from taking the action steps necessary to reach their dreams. A self-directed approach to living and learning modeled by parents for children at home.

The Inner Spa Experience: Innovative Experiential Programs for Progressive Challenging Times
Dorothea Joyce, MA-CMT
Dorothea Joyce Productions
1-888-re-joyce; DorotheaJoyce@aol.com
   "The Inner Spa" is a training program of three to seven days awakening people to the cutting-edge healing modalities of the twenty-first century:

☞ Advanced Energy Healing techniques to teach people to scan their body for areas discordant energies

☞ TransformBreathing and Sound Healing (toning) to connect to, and receive, one's life force through the breath and toning and to release stress and experience joy and a sense of inner well-being

☞ Music therapy for integration of the experience through improvisational playing of music using rhythm and acoustic instruments, including the human voice

☞ Elements of communication through sound, using music as the intermediary for healing and transforming dissonance into harmony

"Pioneering Parenting" programs coach parents and partners in cutting-edge healing modalities before and during the birth experience:

☞ Aromatherapy to sooth and relax

☞ The Triangle Meditation to connect to the baby in inutero before the birth

☞ The benefits of music during birth and upon bringing baby home

☞ Creating a song for baby to entrain it to the new environment

☞ Designing baby's room with Dorothea's Designs

American Music Therapy Association
8455 Colesville Road, Suite 930
Silver Spring, MD 20910
(301) 589-3300

OTHER BOOKS FROM
BEYOND WORDS PUBLISHING, INC.

Nurturing Your Child with Music
How Sound Awareness Creates Happy, Smart, and Confident Children
Author: John M. Ortiz, Ph.D.
$14.95, softcover

Author and psychomusicologist Dr. John Ortiz says that we have "just begun to tap into the powers behind the timeless element of sound," and in his book *Nurturing Your Child with Music*, Dr. Ortiz allows the readers to discover those musical powers through and with their children. Designed for parents who take an active interest in their children's lives, this book offers a number of creative methods through which families can initiate, enhance, and maintain happy, relaxed, and productive home environments. *Nurturing Your Child with Music* includes easy-to-do exercises and fun activities to bring music and sound into parenting styles and family life. The book provides music menus and sample "days of sound" to use during the prenatal, newborn, preschool, and school-age phases. Dr. Ortiz shares how we can keep our family "in tune" and create harmony in our homes by inviting music and sound into our daily dance of life.

Guided Imagery for Healing Children
Author: Ellen Curran, R.N.
$14.95, softcover

The naturally rich imaginations of children are one of the best resources for healing or helping children through difficult times. This book explains how the extraordinary technique of guided imagery can be used as part of a wellness plan for ill or injured children. It introduces the parent/caregiver to the philosophy and science of mind-body medicine and imagery and can also be used by health-care workers, school nurses, home health nurses, physicians, or wellness practitioners.

Discovering Another Way
Raising Brighter Children While Having a Meaningful Career
Author: Lane Nemeth
$16.95, softcover

Discovery Toys is a pioneer in the educational toy market. In *Discovering Another Way*, founder Lane Nemeth tells how she built this $100 million company from the ground up, a company that helped change the lives of tens of thousands of women and an entire generation of kids who have grown up smarter in "Discovery Toys Families." The book provides a refreshingly candid insider's view of how to start your own business and follow your heart, enriching your children's minds and imaginations at the same time. It is also a heartwarming story of Lane Nemeth's dedication to bring quality toys that spark a sense of discovery and learning to all children, not just a chosen few. Interspersed throughout Lane's story are chapters revealing the gems of parenting wisdom she discovered while raising her family and her business: "So You Want a Cooperative Child?," "Guidelines for Brain-Building Play," "How to Turn Your Child into a Lifelong Reader," and "Five Ways to Enhance Your Time with Your Child." Lane explains the magic of learning moments and shows parents how to turn every occasion into an opportunity for discovery and learning.

The Woman's Book of Dreams
Dreaming as a Spiritual Practice
Author: Connie Cockrell Kaplan; Foreword: Jamie Sams
$14.95, softcover

Dreams are the windows to your future and the catalysts to bringing the new and creative into your life. Everyone dreams. Understanding the power of dreaming helps you achieve your greatest potential with ease. *The Woman's Book of Dreams* emphasizes the uniqueness of women's dreaming and shows the reader how to dream with intention, clarity, and focus. In addition, this book will teach you how to recognize the thirteen types of dreams, how your monthly cycles affect your dreaming, how the moon's position in the sky and its relationship to your astrological chart determine your dreaming, and how to track your dreams and create a personal map of your dreaming patterns. Connie Kaplan guides you through an ancient woman's group form called dream circle—a sacred space in which to share dreams with others on a regular basis. Dream circle allows you to experience life's mystery by connecting with other dreamers. It shows you that through dreaming together with your circle, you create the reality in which you live. It is time for you to recognize the power of dreams and to put yours into action. This book will inspire you to do all that—and more.

Teach Only Love
The Twelve Principles of Attitudinal Healing
Author: Gerald G. Jampolsky, M.D.
$12.95, softcover

From best-selling author Dr. Gerald Jampolsky comes a revised and expanded version of one of his classic works, based on *A Course in Miracles*. In 1975, Dr. Jampolsky founded the Center for Attitudinal Healing, a place where children and adults with life-threatening illnesses could practice peace of mind as an instrument of spiritual transformation and inner healing—practices that soon evolved into an approach to life with profound benefits for everyone. This book explains the twelve principles developed at the Center, all of which are based on the healing power of love, forgiveness, and oneness. They provide a powerful guide that allows all of us to heal our relationships and bring peace and harmony to every aspect of our lives.

Forgiveness
The Greatest Healer of All
Author: Gerald G. Jampolsky, M.D.
Foreword: Neale Donald Walsch
$12.95, softcover

Forgiveness: The Greatest Healer of All is written in simple, down-to-earth language. It explains why so many of us find it difficult to forgive and why holding on to grievances is really a decision to suffer. The book describes what causes us to be unforgiving and how our minds work to justify this. It goes on to point out the toxic side effects of being unforgiving and the havoc it can play on our bodies and on our lives. But above all, it leads us to the vast benefits of forgiving.

The author shares powerful stories that open our hearts to the miracles which can take place when we truly believe that no one needs to be excluded from our love. Sprinkled throughout the book are Forgiveness Reminders that may be used as daily affirmations supporting a new life free of past grievances.

Love Sweeter Love
Creating Relationships of Simplicity and Spirit
Author: Jann Mitchell; Foreword: Susan Jeffers
$12.95, softcover

How do we find the time to nurture relationships with the people we love? By simplifying. And *Love Sweeter Love* teaches us how to decide who and what is most important, how to work together as a couple, and how to savor life's sweetest moments. Mitchell has warm, practical, easy-to-understand advice for everyone—young, mature, single, married, or divorced—interested in creating simple, sacred time for love.

Home Sweeter Home
Creating a Haven of Simplicity and Spirit
Author: Jann Mitchell; Foreword: Jack Canfield
$12.95, softcover

We search the world for spirituality and peace—only to discover that happiness and satisfaction are not found "out there" in the world but right here in our houses and in our hearts. Award-winning journalist and author Jann Mitchell offers creative insights and suggestions for making our home life more nurturing, spiritual, and rewarding for ourselves, our families, and our friends.

The Woman's Book of Creativity
Author: C Diane Ealy
$12.95, softcover

Creativity works differently in women and men, and women are most creative when they tap into the process that is unique to their own nature—a holistic, "spiraling" approach. The book is a self-help manual, both inspirational and practical, for igniting female creative fire. Ealy encourages women to acknowledge their own creativity, often in achievements they take for granted. She also gives a wealth of suggestions and exercises to enable women to recognize their own creative power and to access it consistently and effectively. Ealy holds a doctorate in behavioral science and consults with individuals and corporations on creativity.

Rites of Passage
Celebrating Life's Changes
Authors: Kathleen Wall, Ph.D., and Gary Ferguson
$12.95, softcover

Every major transition in our lives—be it marriage, high-school graduation, the death of a parent or spouse, or the last child leaving home—brings with it opportunities for growth and self-actualization and for repositioning ourselves in the world. Personal ritual—the focus of *Rites of Passage*—allows us to use the energy held within the anxiety of change to nourish the new person that is forever struggling to be born. *Rites of Passage* begins by explaining to readers that human growth is not linear, as many of us assume, but rather occurs in a five-part cycle. After sharing the patterns of transition, the authors then show the reader how ritual can help him or her move through these specific life changes: work and career, intimate relationships, friends, divorce, changes within the family, adolescence, issues in the last half of life, and personal loss.

The Intuitive Way

A Guide to Living from Inner Wisdom
Author: Penney Peirce; Foreword: Carol Adrienne
$16.95, softcover

When intuition is in full bloom, life takes on a magical, effortless quality; your world is suddenly full of synchronicities, creative insights, and abundant knowledge just for the asking. *The Intuitive Way* shows you how to enter that state of perceptual aliveness and integrate it into daily life to achieve greater natural flow through an easy-to-understand, ten-step course. Author Penney Peirce synthesizes teachings from psychology, East-West philosophy, religion, metaphysics, and business. In simple and direct language, Peirce describes the intuitive process as a new way of life and demonstrates many practical applications from speeding decision-making to expanding personal growth. Whether you're just beginning to search for a richer, fuller life experience or are looking for more subtle, sophisticated insights about your spiritual path, *The Intuitive Way* will be your companion as you progress through the stages of intuition development.

Every Day God

Heart to Heart with the Divine

Authors: David and Takeko Hose

$14.95, softcover

When Takeko Hose was accidentally shot and paralyzed from the knees down, she and her husband, David, reached out desperately for divine assistance through a succession of what David calls "naked prayers." *Every Day God* is the record of a remarkable communication between authors David and Takeko and God. Not a stickler for ritual, a lofty voice from beyond, or an enigma, their God is a warm and caring parent, eager to nurture and love unconditionally all of His children. Comforting and enlightening, the teachings in *Every Day God* are lighthearted, often humorous, and relevant to modern life. And at the core of each teaching is an invitation to meet this largely undiscovered self within our innermost hearts, a self that flows from our divine source.

The Great Wing

A Parable

Author: Louis A. Tartaglia, M.D.; Foreword: Father Angelo Scolozzi

$14.95, hardcover

The Great Wing transforms the timeless miracle of the migration of a flock of geese into a parable for the modern age. It recounts a young goose's own reluctant but steady transformation from gangly fledgling to Grand Goose, and his triumph over the turmoils of his soul and the buffeting of a mighty Atlantic storm. In *The Great Wing*, our potential as individuals is affirmed, as is the power of group prayer, or the "Flock Mind." As we make the journey with this goose and his flock, we rediscover that we, too, tie our own potential into the power of the common good through honesty, hope, courage, trust, perseverance, spirituality, and service. The young goose's trials and tribulations, as well as his triumph, become our own.

Watermelon Magic

Seeds of Wisdom, Slices of Life

Author: Wally Amos

$14.95, softcover

Watermelon Magic is an inspirational/motivational book using watermelons as a metaphor for life. Utilizing the life experiences of Wally Amos, the book shows the parallels between watermelons and humans. *Watermelon Magic* tells how Wally Amos uses his faith in everyday life and the wisdom gained from the past to help him make wise choices. Just as the vine connects the watermelons, we are all connected by spirit. And just as prickly vines make it difficult to get the melons, our human connections are sometimes prickly, making it difficult for us to achieve our goals and realize our dreams. *Watermelon Magic* helps us acknowledge the difficulties and choose a path to success.

The Girls' Life Guide to Growing Up

By the editors of *Girls' Life* magazine

$11.95, softcover, ages 8–14

The editors of the award-winning *Girls' Life* magazine (readership of two million) have compiled their best advice from issues past and present to offer girls a hip, honest, and street-smart guide to growing up. *The Girls' Life Guide to Growing Up* uses the same direct, funny, and inspiring language and style that girls everywhere have come to know and trust. *Girls' Life* magazine won the 1995 Magazine Launch Award and the 1998 Parent's Choice Award.

Girls Know Best 1, 2, 3

Editors: Michelle Roehm and Marianne Monson-Burton

$8.95, softcover, ages 7–13

Quality advice and activity books real girls can count on because they are written by girls just like them! The series covers topics like siblings, divorce, body image, plus fun activities like slumber party ideas, babysitting brainstorms, and how to analyze your dreams. These books are great ways to encourage girls to use their creativity and to believe in themselves. Winner of the Parent's Council Award and a Scholastic and Book of the Month Club Selection.

To order or to request a catalog, contact

Beyond Words Publishing, Inc.

20827 N.W. Cornell Road, Suite 500

Hillsboro, OR 97124-9808

503-531-8700 or 1-800-284-9673

You can also visit our Web site at *www.beyondword.com* or e-mail us at *info@beyondword.com*.

BEYOND WORDS PUBLISHING, INC.

Our Corporate Mission:

Inspire to Integrity

Our Declared Values:

We give to all of life as life has given us.

We honor all relationships.

Trust and stewardship are integral to fulfilling dreams.

Collaboration is essential to create miracles.

Creativity and aesthetics nourish the soul.

Unlimited thinking is fundamental.

Living your passion is vital.

Joy and humor open our hearts to growth.

It is important to remind ourselves of love.